Topps® BASEBA

are published by

PRICE STERN SLOAN

There is a Topps® BASEBALL CARD BOOK for every major league team. Collect them all or concentrate on your favorites.

NEW YORK Yankees

Available for all 26 teams!

Topps® BASEBALL CARD BOOKS are available wherever books or baseball cards are sold, or may be ordered directly from the publisher. Simply send your check or money order for $9.95 plus $2.00 for shipping and handling to—

PRICE STERN SLOAN
Cash Sales
360 North La Cienega Boulevard
Los Angeles, CA 90048

You'll find books for all 26 major league teams at the Topps® BOOKS HEADQUARTERS STORE. To locate the HEADQUARTERS nearest you, simply call:

PRICE STERN SLOAN
(800) 421-0892
Calling from CA (800) 227-8801

Topps

BASEBALL CARDS

NEW YORK Yankees

Text by

Red Foley

PRICE STERN SLOAN
Los Angeles

Published by Price Stern Sloan, Inc.
360 North La Cienega Boulevard, Los Angeles, California 90048

ISBN 0-8431-2466-0

An MBKA Production

Printed and bound in Hong Kong .

TEAM LEADERS

Hall of Famers

Frank "Home Run" Baker
Ed Barrow (Executive)
Yogi Berra
Frank Chance
Jack Chesbro
Earle Combs
Stan Coveleski
Bill Dickey
Joe DiMaggio
Whitey Ford
Lou Gehrig
Lefty Gomez
Clark Griffith
Burleigh Grimes
Bucky Harris (Manager)
Waite Hoyt
Miller Huggins (Manager)
Jim "Catfish" Hunter
Willie Keeler
Larry MacPhail (Executive)
Mickey Mantle
Joe McCarthy (Manager)
Bill McKechnie (Manager)
Johnny Mize
Herb Pennock
Branch Rickey
Red Ruffing
Babe Ruth
Joe Sewell
Enos Slaughter
Casey Stengel (Manager)
Dazzy Vance
Paul Waner
George Weiss (Executive)

No-Hitters

8-30-10 Tom Hughes (vs. Indians)
4-24-17 George Mogridge (at Boston)
9-04-23 Sam Jones (at Philadelphia)
8-27-38 Monte Pearson (vs. Indians)
7-12-51 Allie Reynolds (at Cleveland)
9-28-51 Allie Reynolds (vs. Red Sox)
*10-08-56 Don Larsen (vs. Dodgers)
7-04-83 Dave Righetti (vs. Red Sox)

*Perfect Game in World Series.

Twenty Game Winners

1903 - Jack Chesbro (21)
1904 - Jack Chesbro (41)
Jack Powell (23)
1906 - Al Orth (27)
Jack Chesbro (24)
1910 - Russ Ford (26)
1911 - Russ Ford (22)
1916 - Bob Shawkey (23)
1919 - Bob Shawkey (20)
1920 - Carl Mays (26)
Bob Shawkey (20)
1921 - Carl Mays (27)
1922 - Joe Bush (26)
Bob Shawkey (20)
1923 - Sam Jones (21)
1924 - Herb Pennock (21)
1926 - Herb Pennock (23)
1927 - Waite Hoyt (22)
1928 - George Pipgras (24)
Waite Hoyt (23)
1931 - Lefty Gomez (21)
1932 - Lefty Gomez (24)
1934 - Lefty Gomez (26)
1936 - Red Ruffing (20)
1937 - Lefty Gomez (21)
Red Ruffing (20)
1938 - Red Ruffing (21)
1939 - Red Ruffing (21)
1942 - Ernie Bonham (21)
1943 - Spud Chandler (20)
*1945 - Hank Borowy (21)
1946 - Spud Chandler (20)
1949 - Vic Raschi (21)
1950 - Vic Raschi (21)
1951 - Eddie Lopat (21)
Vic Raschi (21)
1952 - Allie Reynolds (20)
1954 - Bob Grim (20)
1958 - Bob Turley (21)
1961 - Whitey Ford (25)
1962 - Ralph Terry (23)
1963 - Whitey Ford (24)
Jim Bouton (21)
1965 - Mel Stottlemyre (20)
1968 - Mel Stottlemyre (21)
1969 - Mel Stottlemyre (20)
1970 - Fritz Peterson (20)
1975 - Jim "Catfish" Hunter (23)
1978 - Ron Guidry (25)
Ed Figueroa (20)
1979 - Tommy John (21)
1980 - Tommy John (22)
1983 - Ron Guidry (21)
1985 - Ron Guidry (22)

*Pitched with Yankees (10) and Cubs (11).

League Leaders

Batting Average
1924 - Babe Ruth (.378)
1934 - Lou Gehrig (.363)
1939 - Joe DiMaggio (.381)
1940 - Joe DiMaggio (.352)
1945 - George Stirnweiss (.309)
1956 - Mickey Mantle (.353)
1984 - Don Mattingly (.343)

Runs Batted In
1916 - Wally Pipp (99)
1920 - Babe Ruth (137)
1921 - Babe Ruth (171)
1923 - Babe Ruth (131)
1925 - Bob Meusel (138)
1926 - Babe Ruth (145)
1927 - Lou Gehrig (175)
1928 - Lou Gehrig,
Babe Ruth (142)
1930 - Lou Gehrig (174)
1931 - Lou Gehrig (184)
1934 - Lou Gehrig (165)
1941 - Joe DiMaggio (125)
1945 - Nick Etten (111)
1948 - Joe DiMaggio (155)
1956 - Mickey Mantle (130)
1960 - Roger Maris (112)
1961 - Roger Maris (142)
1985 - Don Mattingly (145)

Home Runs
1916 - Wally Pipp (12)
1917 - Wally Pipp (9)
1920 - Babe Ruth (54)
1921 - Babe Ruth (59)
1923 - Babe Ruth (41)
1924 - Babe Ruth (46)
1925 - Bob Meusel (33)
1926 - Babe Ruth (47)
1927 - Babe Ruth (60)
1928 - Babe Ruth (54)
1929 - Babe Ruth (46)
1930 - Babe Ruth (49)
*1931 - Lou Gehrig,
Babe Ruth (46)
1934 - Lou Gehrig (49)
1936 - Lou Gehrig (49)
1937 - Joe DiMaggio (46)
1944 - Nick Etten (22)
1948 - Joe DiMaggio (39)
1955 - Mickey Mantle (37)
1956 - Mickey Mantle (52)
1958 - Mickey Mantle (42)
1960 - Mickey Mantle (40)
1961 - Roger Maris (61)
1976 - Graig Nettles (32)
*1980 - Reggie Jackson (41)

*Tied

Strikeouts
1932 - Red Ruffing (190)
1933 - Lefty Gomez (163)
1934 - Lefty Gomez (158)
1937 - Lefty Gomez (194)
1951 - Vic Raschi (164)
1952 - Allie Reynolds (160)
1964 - Al Downing (217)

Wins
1904 - Jack Chesbro (41)
1906 - Al Orth (27)
*1921 - Carl Mays (27)
*1927 - Waite Hoyt (22)
*1928 - George Pipgras (24)
1934 - Lefty Gomez (26)
1937 - Lefty Gomez (21)
1938 - Red Ruffing (21)
*1943 - Spud Chandler (20)
*1955 - Whitey Ford (18)
1958 - Bob Turley (21)
1961 - Whitey Ford (25)
1962 - Ralph Terry (23)
1963 - Whitey Ford (24)
*1975 - Jim "Catfish" Hunter (23)
1978 - Ron Guidry (25)
1985 - Ron Guidry (22)

*Tied

Earned Run Average
1920 - Bob Shawkey (2.45)
1927 - Wilcy Moore (2.28)
1934 - Lefty Gomez (2.33)
1943 - Spud Chandler (1.64)
1947 - Spud Chandler (2.46)
1952 - Allie Reynolds (2.07)
1953 - Eddie Lopat (2.43)
1956 - Whitey Ford (2.47)
1957 - Bobby Shantz (2.45)
1958 - Whitey Ford (2.01)
1978 - Ron Guidry (1.74)
1979 - Ron Guidry (2.78)
1980 - Rudy May (2.47)

Cy Young Award Winners
1958 - Bob Turley
1961 - Whitey Ford
1977 - Sparky Lyle
1978 - Ron Guidry

Most Valuable Players
1923 - Babe Ruth
1927 - Lou Gehrig
1936 - Lou Gehrig
1939 - Joe DiMaggio
1941 - Joe DiMaggio
1942 - Joe Gordon
1943 - Spud Chandler
1947 - Joe DiMaggio
1950 - Phil Rizzuto
1951 - Yogi Berra
1954 - Yogi Berra
1955 - Yogi Berra
1956 - Mickey Mantle
1957 - Mickey Mantle
1960 - Roger Maris
1961 - Roger Maris
1962 - Mickey Mantle
1963 - Elston Howard
1976 - Thurman Munson
1985 - Don Mattingly

World Series Appearances

1921	*1941	1957
1922	1942	*1958
*1923	*1943	1960
1926	*1947	*1961
*1927	*1949	*1962
*1928	*1950	1963
*1932	*1951	1964
*1936	*1952	1976
*1937	*1953	*1977
*1938	1955	*1978
*1939	*1956	1981

*World Champions

Compiled by Bill Haber.

1952

It was, like so many years that preceded it, a fruitful season for the Yankees. They not only won their fourth straight American League flag, in 1952, this one by two lengths over Cleveland, but topped it with victory over the Brooklyn Dodgers in a seven-game World Series.

Despite a shoulder problem for lefthander Eddie Lopat, plus Korean War inductions of Jerry Coleman, Bobby Brown and Tom Morgan, Allie Reynolds won 20 games and led the league with a 2.07 earned run average.

Sophomore Mickey Mantle batted .311 and hit 23 home runs, while Yogi Berra slugged 30 four-baggers and had 98 runs batted in, both records for American League catchers.

JOHNNY HOPP

RALPH HOUK
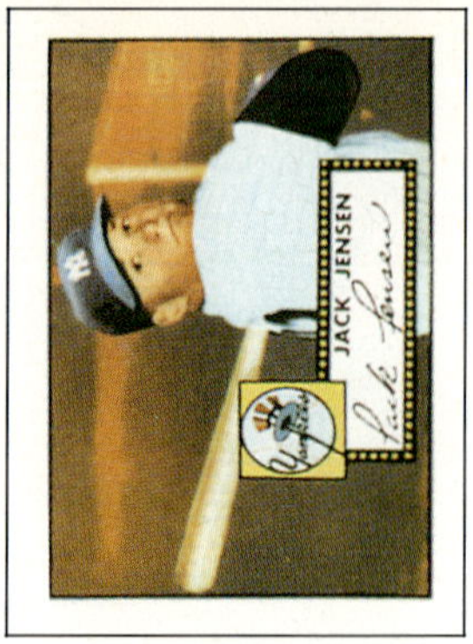
JACK JENSEN

BOB KUZAVA

ED LOPAT

MICKEY MANTLE

BILLY MARTIN

GIL McDOUGALD

BILL MILLER
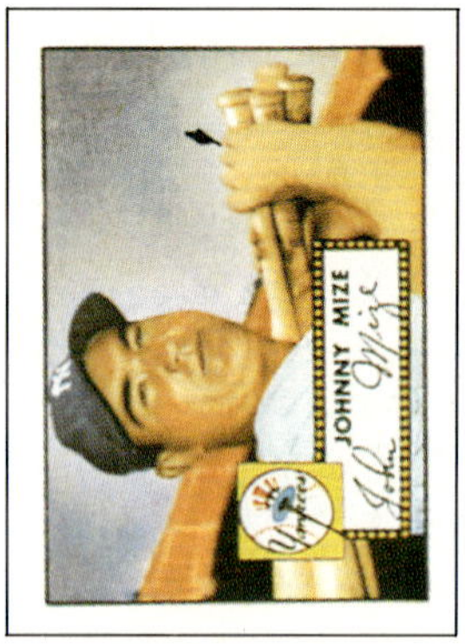
JOHNNY MIZE

TOM MORGAN

JOE OSTROWSKI

FRANK OVERMIRE

JOE PAGE

ALLIE REYNOLDS

PHIL RIZZUTO

1953

An unprecedented fifth straight American League pennant and World Series victory (over the Dodgers) was the Yankees' story in 1953. For Casey Stengel it was the easiest of his triumphal string, finishing eight and a half games in front of the pursuing Cleveland Indians.

The Yankees all but clinched their flag in late May when they launched an 18-game winning streak. Outfielder Hank Bauer, at .304, was the club's top hitter, while Yogi Berra paced the club in home runs (27) and RBIs (108).

Though failing to produce a 20-game winner for the first time since 1948, the Yankees celebrated a mound staff that was numerically the best in the league. Lefthander Whitey Ford, back following two years of military service, was the team's top winner with 18, while veteran Eddie Lopat, recovered from a shoulder ailment that idled him much of the 1952 season, rebounded with a 16-4 record and his 2.43 ERA was the best in the league.

Yankees
YOGI BERRA
catcher NEW YORK YANKEES

Yankees
Ewell BLACKWELL
pitcher NEW YORK YANKEES

Yankees
ANDY CAREY
infielder NEW YORK YANKEES

Yankees
BOB CERV
outfielder NEW YORK YANKEES

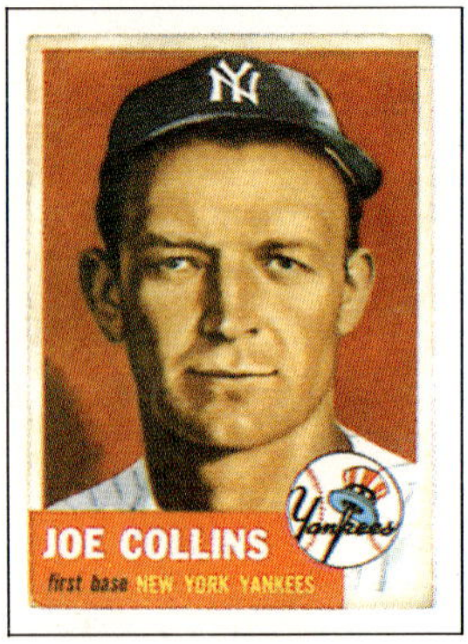
Yankees
JOE COLLINS
first base NEW YORK YANKEES

Yankees
WHITEY FORD
pitcher NEW YORK YANKEES

Yankees
ED LOPAT
pitcher NEW YORK YANKEES

Yankees
MICKEY MANTLE
outfielder NEW YORK YANKEES

Yankees
BILLY MARTIN
second base NEW YORK YANKEES

Yankees
GIL McDOUGALD
third base NEW YORK YANKEES

Yankees
BILL MILLER
pitcher NEW YORK YANKEES

Yankees
JOHN MIZE
first base NEW YORK YANKEES

Yankees
TOM MORGAN
pitcher NEW YORK YANKEES

Yankees
IRV NOREN
outfielder NEW YORK YANKEES

Yankees
ALLIE REYNOLDS
pitcher NEW YORK YANKEES

Yankees
PHIL RIZZUTO
shortstop NEW YORK YANKEES

1954

It was a year the Yankees did everything but win the American League pennant. They won 103 games, the most by any Yankees club managed by Casey Stengel, but the Bombers still finished eight lengths behind Cleveland which won a league-record 111 games.

The Yankees' .268 batting average was the best in the league, and rookie righthander Bob Grim won 20 games. Yogi Berra, Mickey Mantle, Irv Noren and Andy Carey were the Bombers' .300 hitters and both Berra (125) and Mantle (102) achieved the century plateau in runs batted in.

Despite edging to within a game and a half of Cleveland in early September, the Yankees' bid for flag No. 6 failed when the Tribe won 11 in a row, including a big doubleheader sweep over the visiting Yankees, Sept. 12, in Cleveland.

HANK BAUER
outfield NEW YORK YANKEES

YOGI BERRA
catcher NEW YORK YANKEES

ANDY CAREY
third base NEW YORK YANKEES

JOE COLLINS
first base NEW YORK YANKEES

WHITEY FORD
pitcher NEW YORK YANKEES

BOB KUZAVA
pitcher NEW YORK YANKEES

FRANK LEJA
first base NEW YORK YANKEES

ED LOPAT
pitcher NEW YORK YANKEES
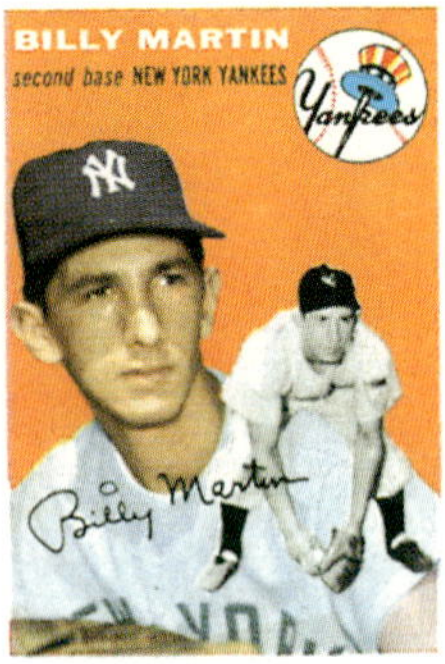
BILLY MARTIN
second base NEW YORK YANKEES

WILLIE MIRANDA
shortstop NEW YORK YANKEES

PHIL RIZZUTO
shortstop NEW YORK YANKEES

EDDIE ROBINSON
first base NEW YORK YANKEES
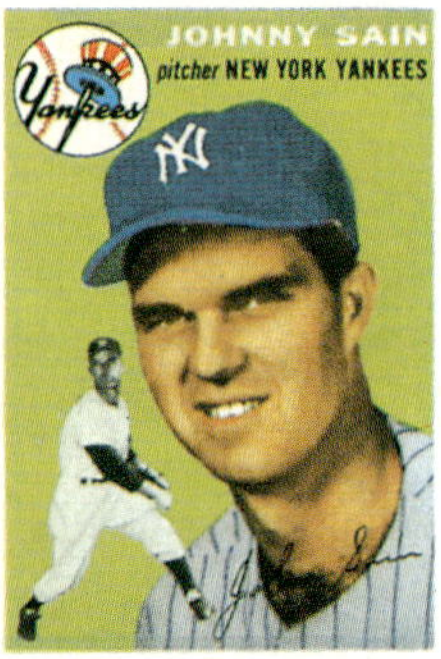
JOHNNY SAIN
pitcher NEW YORK YANKEES

CHARLIE SILVERA
catcher NEW YORK YANKEES

BILL SKOWRON
first base NEW YORK YANKEES

GENE WOODLING
outfield NEW YORK YANKEES

1955

Only a loss in seven games to the Brooklyn Dodgers in the World Series scarred what was another outstanding season for the Yankees in 1955. What had been a four club race, with Cleveland, Boston and Chicago challenging the Bombers in the second half, became academic when Casey Stengel's club won 15 of their last 19 games to finish three lengths ahead of the Indians.

Mickey Mantle and Bill Skowron were the Yankees' .300 hitters and the Mick's 37 homers led the American League. Yogi Berra, despite a mere .272 batting average, banged 27 homers and led the club with 108 RBIs and was again acclaimed the league's Most Valuable Player.

Whitey Ford was the staff's biggest winner with 18, while veteran lefthander Tommy Byrne chipped in with a 16-5 season to help offset the retirement of longtime pitching ace Allie Reynolds.

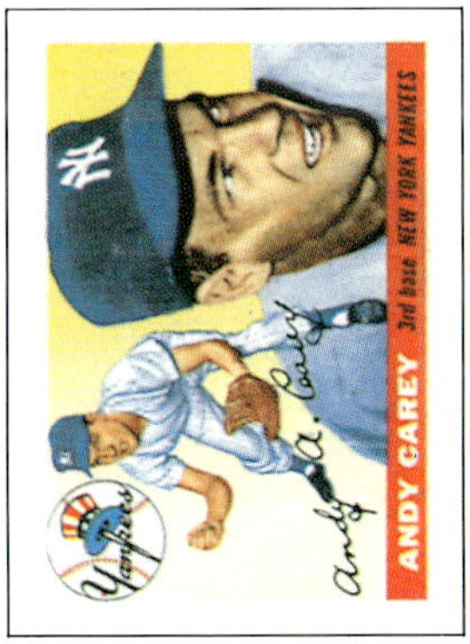

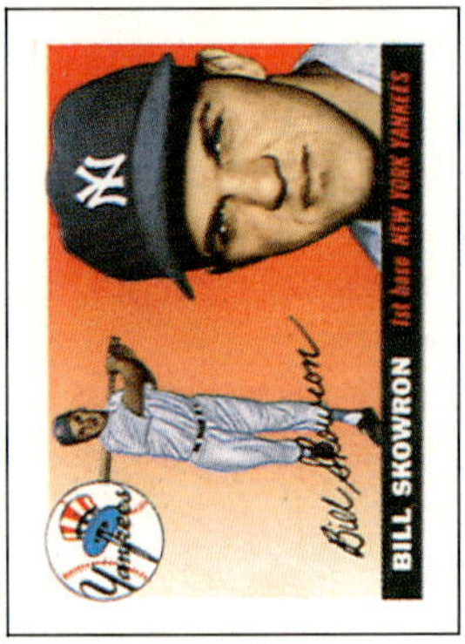

1956

Mickey Mantle's Triple Crown — batting average, home runs and runs batted in — plus his Most Valuable Player award, spearheaded the Yankees' second successive American League flag.

Then, as they'd done so often in the past, the Bombers defeated the Brooklyn Dodgers, in a seven-game World Series that was punctuated by Don Larsen's perfect no-hit, no-run achievement in Game No. 5.

The Yankees took the league lead permanently in mid-May and finished nine games up on Cleveland. As a team the Yankees set a league record with 190 homers, 52 of them from Mantle's awesome bat. His .353 average was the best and his 130 RBIs made him only the ninth player in major league annals to gain the batting triad.

Whitey Ford, with 19 victories, led the staff and his 2.47 ERA paced the league. Johnny Kucks and Tom Sturdivant, neither of whom was prominent in the early season mound blueprint, chipped in with 18 and 16 wins, respectively.

JOHNNY KUCKS
pitcher NEW YORK YANKEES

"WHITEY" FORD
pitcher NEW YORK YANKEES

TOMMY CARROLL
shortstop NEW YORK YANKEES

HANK BAUER
outfield NEW YORK YANKEES

DON LARSEN
pitcher NEW YORK YANKEES

BOB GRIM
pitcher NEW YORK YANKEES

BOB CERV
outfield NEW YORK YANKEES

YOGI BERRA
catcher NEW YORK YANKEES

MICKEY MANTLE
outfield NEW YORK YANKEES

ELSTON HOWARD
catcher-o.f. NEW YORK YANKEES

JERRY COLEMAN
infield NEW YORK YANKEES

TOMMY BYRNE
pitcher NEW YORK YANKEES

BILLY MARTIN
2b-shortstop N. Y. YANKEES

JIM KONSTANTY
pitcher NEW YORK YANKEES

JOE COLLINS
first base NEW YORK YANKEES

ANDY CAREY
third base NEW YORK YANKEES

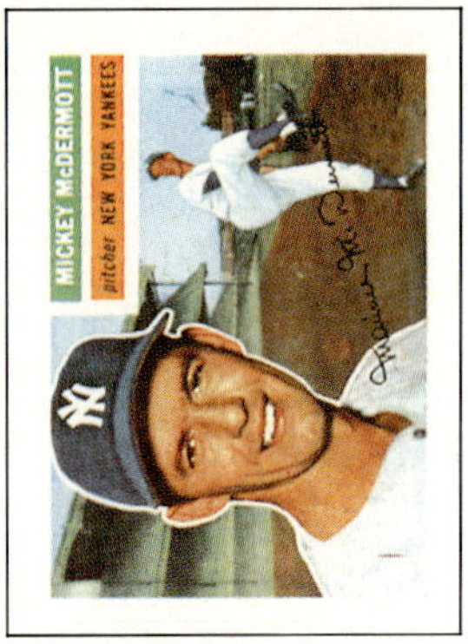

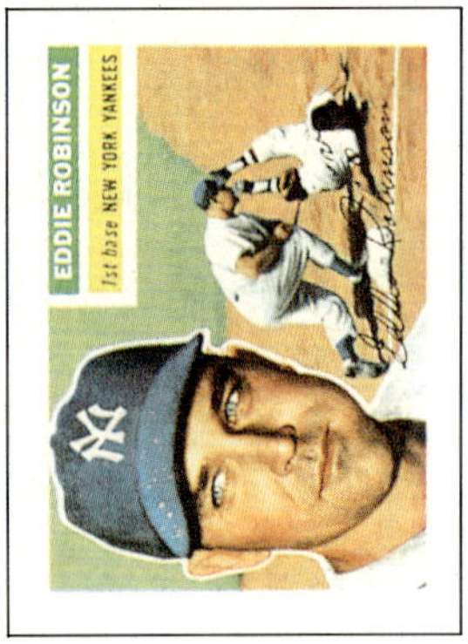

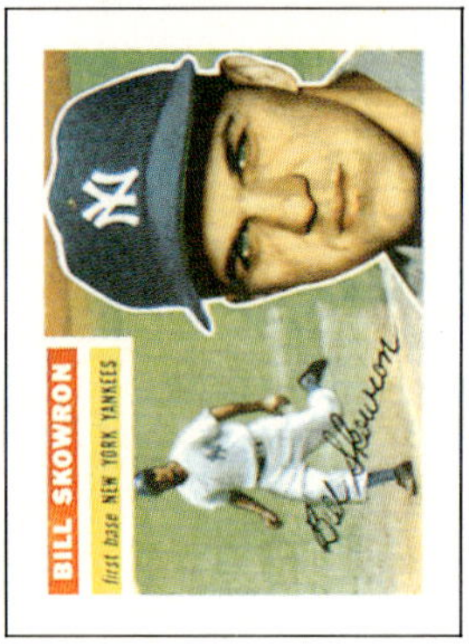

1957

It required some of manager Casey Stengel's famed juggling to do it, but the Yankees achieved their eighth American League flag in nine seasons in 1957. They finished eight games atop the pursuing Chicago White Sox, but it wasn't until September the Bombers finally locked it up.

Mickey Mantle, the MVP for the second straight year, batted .365 and hit 34 homers and had 94 RBIs despite a series of nagging injuries. Bill Skowron contributed to the offense with a .304 average and 88 runs batted in as the Yankees led the league with a .268 average and a 3.00 earned run average. Tony Kubek, playing five positions, hit .297 and earned Rookie of the Year honors.

The staff didn't produce a 20-game winner, but Stengel had six hurlers win 10 or more with Tom Sturdivant's 16 tops for the moundsmen. Bob Turley followed him with 13. The lone blot on the Yankees' season was their loss to the Milwaukee Braves in seven games in a World Series in which assorted ailments restricted Mantle and fellow slugger Skowron.

HANK Bauer
N. Y. YANKEES OUTFIELD

YOGI Berra
NEW YORK YANKEES CATCHER

TOMMY Byrne
NEW YORK YANKEES PITCHER

ANDY Carey
N. Y. YANKEES THIRD BASE

TOMMY Carroll
N. Y. YANKEES SHORTSTOP

AL Cicotte
YANKEES PITCHER

JERRY Coleman
N. Y. YANKEES INFIELD

JOE Collins
N. Y. YANKEES 1st B. - O.F.

ART Ditmar
N. Y. YANKEES PITCHER

WHITEY Ford
NEW YORK YANKEES PITCHER

BOB Grim
NEW YORK YANKEES PITCHER

Howard
N. Y. YANKEES

DARRELL Johnson
N. Y. YANKEES CATCHER

TONY Kubek
N. Y. YANKEES OUTFIELD

JOHNNY Kucks
N. Y. YANKEES PITCHER

DON Larsen
NEW YORK YANKEES PITCHER

MICKEY Mantle
N. Y. YANKEES OUTFIELD

BILLY Martin
N. Y. YANKEES 2nd BASE

GIL McDougald
N. Y. YANKEES SHORTSTOP

BOBBY Richardson
N. Y. YANKEES 2nd B.-S.S.

BOBBY Shantz
N. Y. YANKEES PITCHER
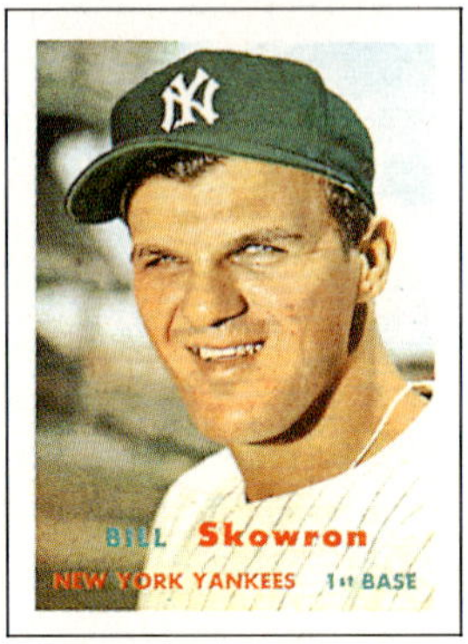
BILL Skowron
NEW YORK YANKEES 1st BASE

ENOS Slaughter
N. Y. YANKEES OUTFIELD

TOM Sturdivant
NEW YORK YANKEES PITCHER

RALPH Terry
N. Y. YANKEES PITCHER

BOB Turley
N. Y. YANKEES PITCHER

Yankees' Power Hitters
MANTLE BERRA

NEW YORK YANKEES

1958

The Yankees captured the 1958 American League pennant by 11 games and except for a late-season slump might even have doubled that victorious margin. It was their ninth flag in 10 seasons and it enabled Casey Stengel to tie Connie Mack and Joe McCarthy in pennants won by a manager.

Bob Turley, with a 21-7 mark, was the league's lone 20-game winner and received the Cy Young Award as the game's top pitcher. The Yankees' staff posted a league-leading 3.22 ERA.

Whitey Ford, 14-7, was restricted by injuries, but his 2.01 ERA was sufficient to lead the league and his seven shutouts also paced the league's pitchers. Rookie Ryne Duren, one of the game's hardest throwers, emerged as the club's bullpen star, striking out 87 in the 76 innings he worked while making 43 relief appearances.

Despite lingering shoulder problems, which reduced his average to .304, Mickey Mantle hit 42 homers to again lead the league. Elston Howard, at .314, and Norm Siebern, at .300, were the other Yankees to reach the charmed circle. What put the frosting on the Yankees' cake was their comeback from a 1-3 deficit to defeat Milwaukee in a seven-game World Series.

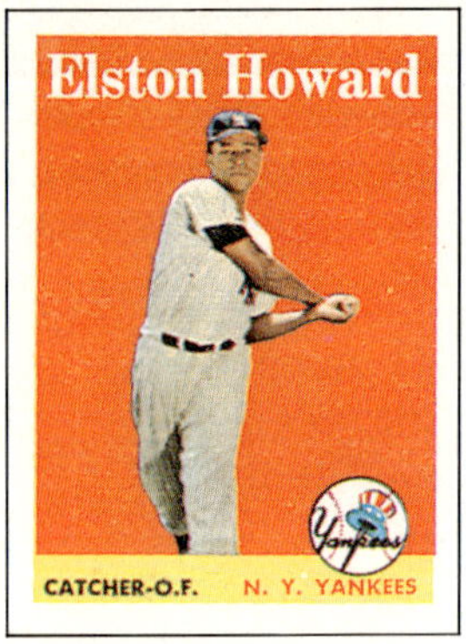
Elston Howard
CATCHER-O.F.
N. Y. YANKEES

Darrell Johnson
CATCHER
NEW YORK YANKEES
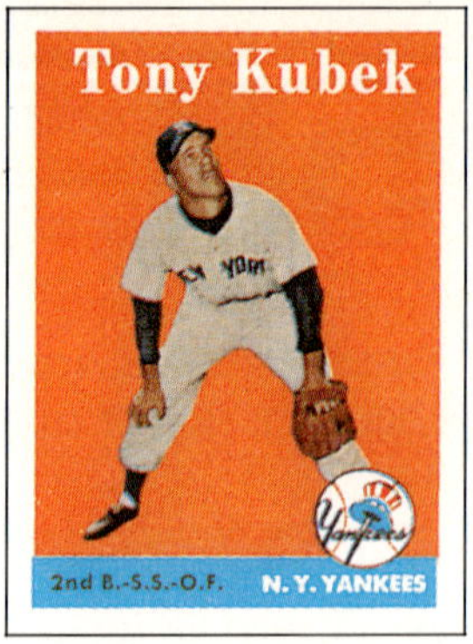
Tony Kubek
2nd B.-S.S.-O.F.
N. Y. YANKEES

Johnny Kucks
PITCHER
NEW YORK YANKEES

Don Larsen
PITCHER
NEW YORK YANKEES

Jerry Lumpe
3rd Base-O.F.
N. Y. YANKEES

Sal Maglie
PITCHER
NEW YORK YANKEES

Mickey Mantle
OUTFIELD
NEW YORK YANKEES

SPORT Magazine
'58 ALL STAR Selection
MICKEY MANTLE
CENTER FIELD • AMERICAN LEAGUE

Gil McDougald
SHORTSTOP
N.Y. YANKEES

Bobby Richardson
2nd B.
NEW YORK YANKEES

Bobby Shantz
PITCHER
NEW YORK YANKEES

Norm Siebern
OUTFIELD
NEW YORK YANKEES

Harry Simpson
1st B.-O.F.
N. Y. YANKEES

SPORT Magazine
'58 ALL STAR Selection
BILL SKOWRON
FIRST BASE • AMERICAN LEAGUE

Moose Skowron
1st BASE
NEW YORK YANKEES

1959

The Yankees, for only the second time in the decade, failed to claim the American League pennant: they finished third, 15 games behind the victorious Chicago White Sox. The Bombers, never really in the hunt, spent 11 days in the league cellar in late May and were a second division club for almost half the season.

Bob Turley, a 21-game winner in 1958, posted a dismal 8-11 log and his ERA zoomed from 2.97 to 4.32. Don Larsen, 6-1 in the early going, didn't win another game after June 13 and finished 6-7. Art Ditmar, 13-9, and Whitey Ford, 16-10, were the Yankees' most productive hurlers.

Bobby Richardson, at .301, was the club's lone .300 batsman, while Bill Skowron, idled by a fractured left wrist on July 25, finished at .298. The injury-plagued Mickey Mantle hit 31 homers, had 75 RBIs and batted .285.

hank bauer
NEW YORK YANKEES
OUTFIELD

yogi berra
NEW YORK YANKEES
CATCHER

The Sporting News
ROOKIE STARS OF 1959
JOHN BLANCHARD
YANKEES CATCHER

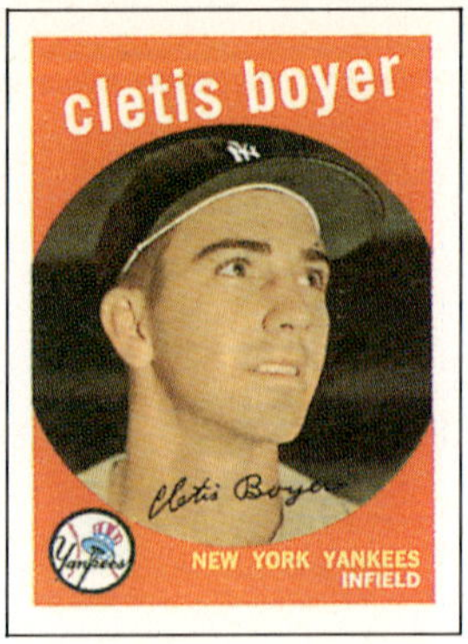
cletis boyer
NEW YORK YANKEES
INFIELD

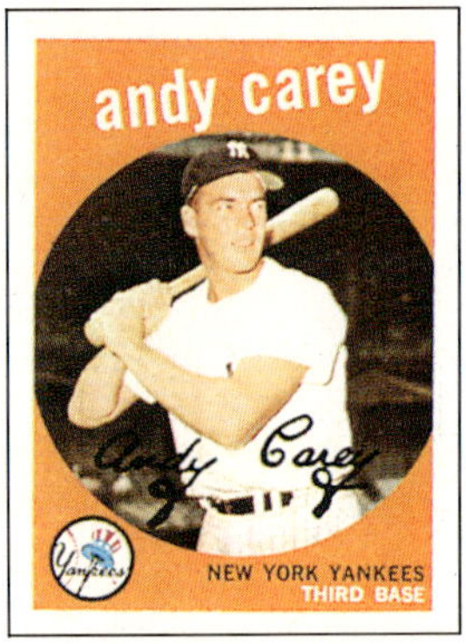
andy carey
NEW YORK YANKEES
THIRD BASE

jim coates
NEW YORK YANKEES
PITCHER

murry dickson
NEW YORK YANKEES
PITCHER

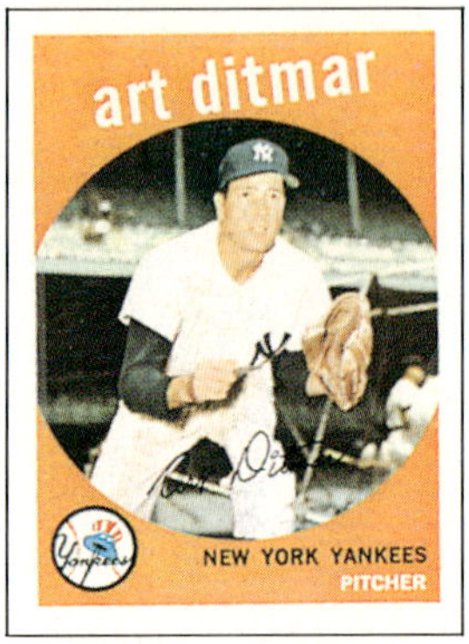
art ditmar
NEW YORK YANKEES
PITCHER

ryne duren
NEW YORK YANKEES
PITCHER

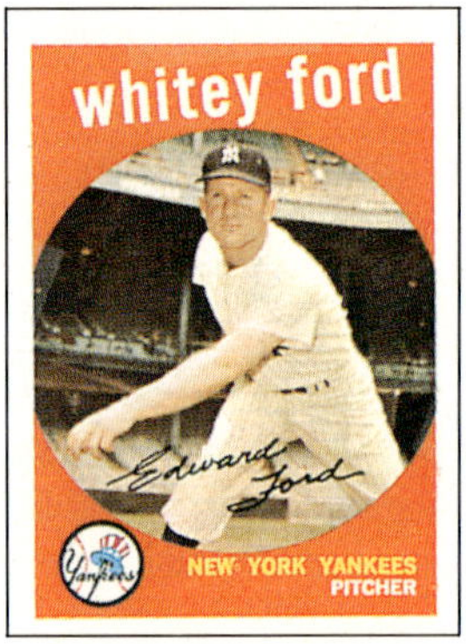
whitey ford
NEW YORK YANKEES
PITCHER

elston howard
NEW YORK YANKEES
CATCHER—OUTFIELD

darrell johnson
NEW YORK YANKEES
CATCHER

The Sporting News
ROOKIE STARS OF 1959
DERON JOHNSON
YANKEES OUTFIELD

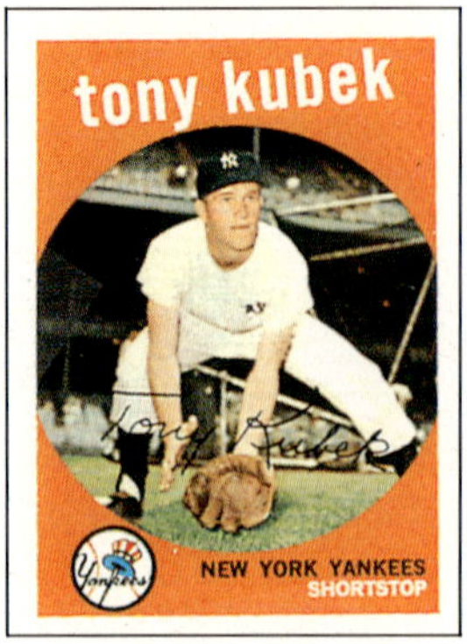
tony kubek
NEW YORK YANKEES
SHORTSTOP

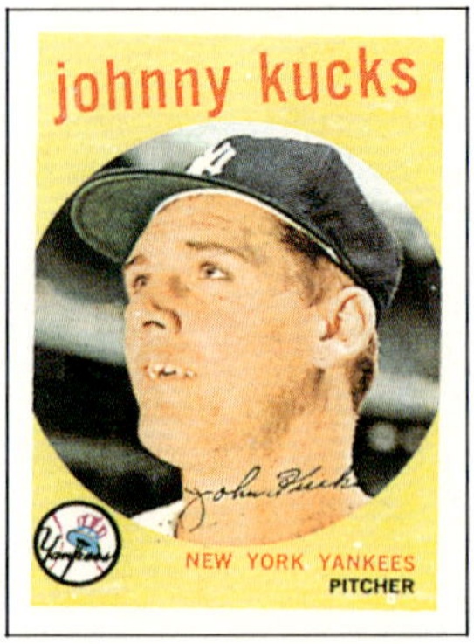
johnny kucks
NEW YORK YANKEES
PITCHER

don larsen
NEW YORK YANKEES
PITCHER

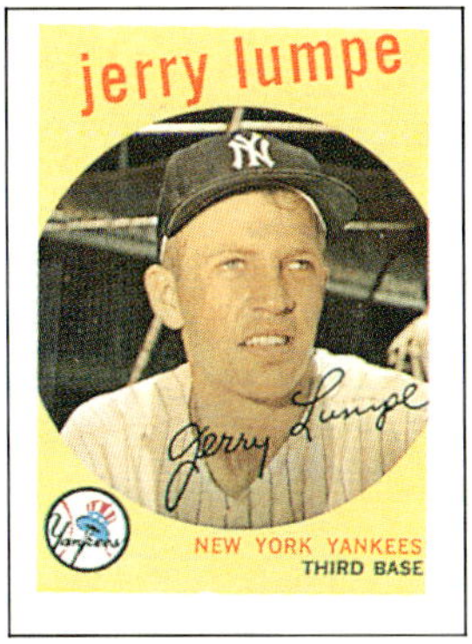
jerry lumpe
NEW YORK YANKEES
THIRD BASE
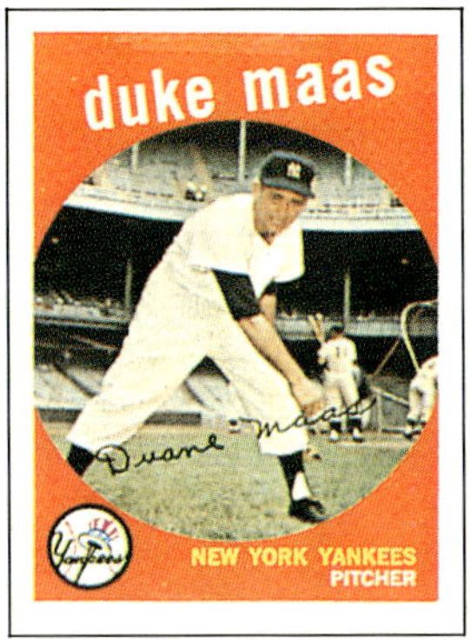
duke maas
NEW YORK YANKEES
PITCHER

mickey mantle
NEW YORK YANKEES
OUTFIELD

The Sporting News
MICKEY MANTLE
CENTER FIELD AMERICAN LEAGUE
'59 ALL STAR SELECTION
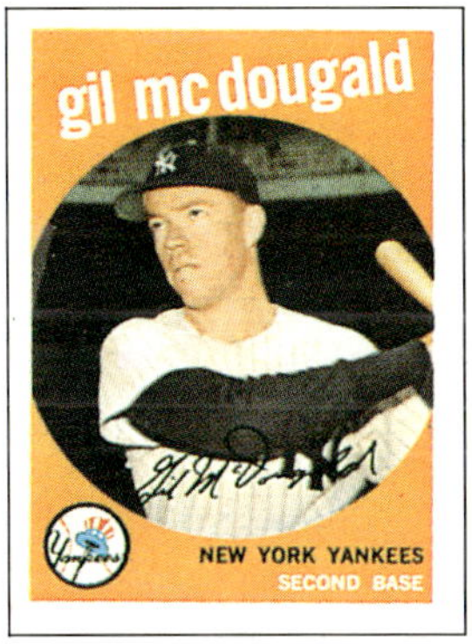
gil mc dougald
NEW YORK YANKEES
SECOND BASE

zack monroe
NEW YORK YANKEES
PITCHER
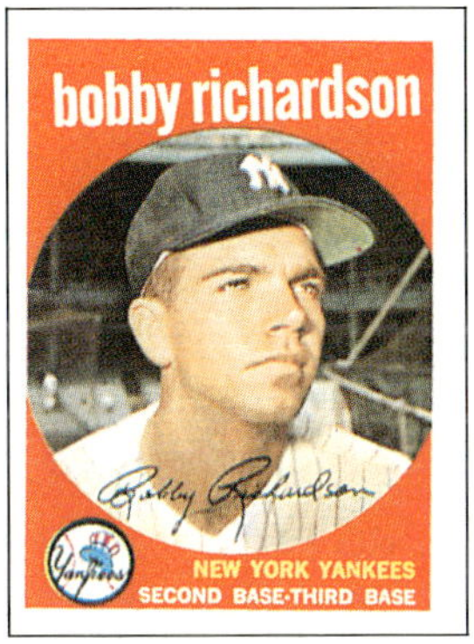
bobby richardson
NEW YORK YANKEES
SECOND BASE-THIRD BASE
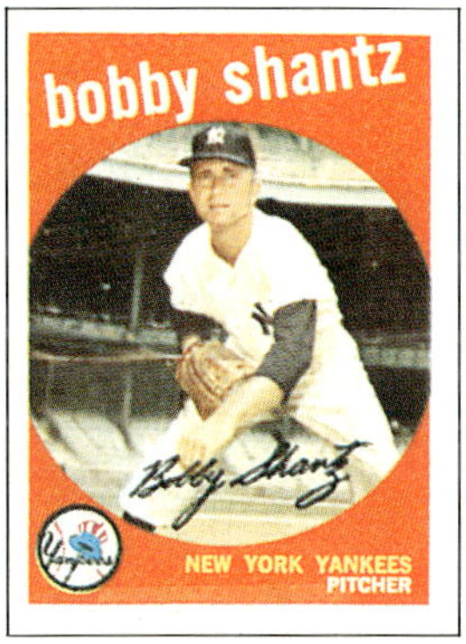
bobby shantz
NEW YORK YANKEES
PITCHER

norm siebern
NEW YORK YANKEES
OUTFIELD
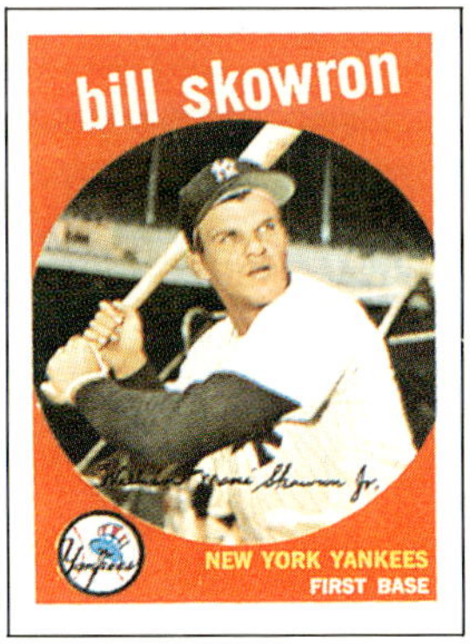
bill skowron
NEW YORK YANKEES
FIRST BASE

The Sporting News
BILL SKOWRON
FIRST BASE AMERICAN LEAGUE
'59 ALL STAR SELECTION
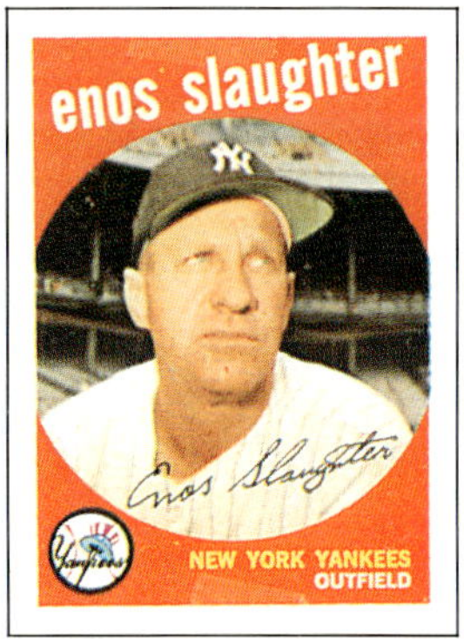
enos slaughter
NEW YORK YANKEES
OUTFIELD

The Sporting News
CASEY STENGEL
MANAGER AMERICAN LEAGUE
'59 ALL STAR SELECTION

tom sturdivant
NEW YORK YANKEES
PITCHER

marv throneberry
NEW YORK YANKEES
FIRST BASE—OUTFIELD
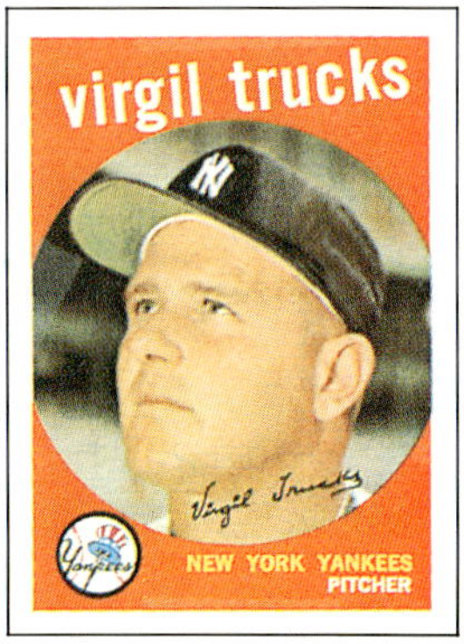
virgil trucks
NEW YORK YANKEES
PITCHER

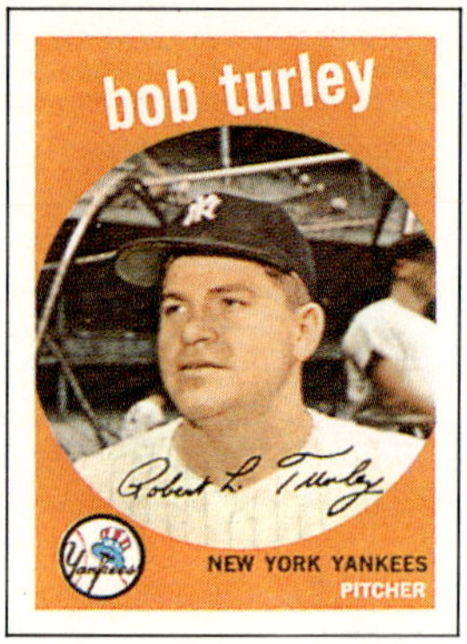

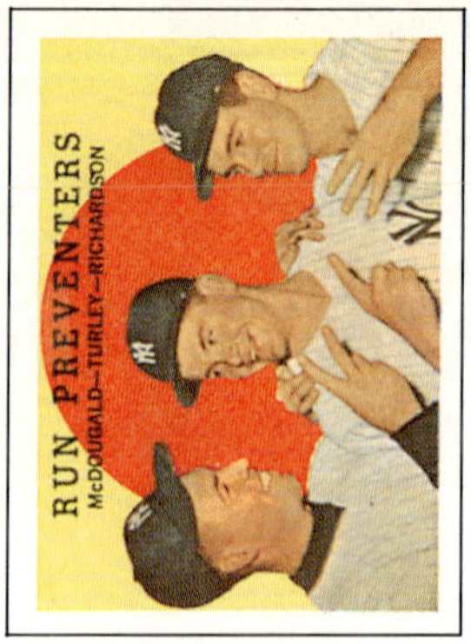

1960

The 1960s began as did the 1950s — with Casey Stengel and the Yankees winning the American League pennant. But this time they failed to add a World Series victory, dropping a seven-game set to the Pittsburgh Pirates.

Shortly after, they dropped the 70-year-old Stengel, who in his dozen seasons at the club's helm won a record-tying 10 flags and added eight Series triumphs. In what was Stengel's valedictory season the Yankees, winning 19 of their final 21 games, romped home eight lengths ahead of the Baltimore Orioles.

Mickey Mantle and Roger Maris, acquired from Kansas City, combined for 79 home runs as the Yankees set a league mark with 193. Maris, with a .283 average, hit 39 homers and led the league with 112 RBIs and was voted the Most Valuable Player. Mantle, despite batting .275, led the league with 40 homers and had 94 RBIs.

The lack of a dominant pitcher didn't faze Stengel as he maneuvered a less than spectacular staff that was led by Art Ditmar's 15 wins. Whitey Ford was 12-9 and Jim Coates, who won nine in a row, finished with 13-3. Veteran lefty Luis Arroyo, promoted from the minors in July, was 5-1 out of the bullpen.

KEN HUNT
NEW YORK YANKEES
OUTFIELD

WHITEY FORD
NEW YORK YANKEES
PITCHER

JIM COATES
NEW YORK YANKEES
PITCHER

YOGI BERRA
NEW YORK YANKEES
CATCHER

JOHNNY JAMES
NEW YORK YANKEES
PITCHER

ELI GRBA
NEW YORK YANKEES
PITCHER

JOE DE MAESTRI
NEW YORK YANKEES
SHORTSTOP

JOHN BLANCHARD
NEW YORK YANKEES
CATCHER

SPORT MAGAZINE
1960
ROOKIE
STAR
DERON JOHNSON
N.Y. YANKEES
Outfield

KENT HADLEY
NEW YORK YANKEES
FIRST BASE

ART DITMAR
NEW YORK YANKEES
PITCHER

CLETIS BOYER
NEW YORK YANKEES
SHORTSTOP

TONY KUBEK
NEW YORK YANKEES
SHORTSTOP-OUTFIELD

ELSTON HOWARD
N. Y. YANKEES
CATCHER-OUTFIELD-1B

RYNE DUREN
NEW YORK YANKEES
PITCHER

ANDY CAREY
NEW YORK YANKEES
THIRD BASE

HECTOR LOPEZ
OUTFIELD
NEW YORK YANKEES
DUKE MAAS
PITCHER
NEW YORK YANKEES
MICKEY MANTLE
OUTFIELD
NEW YORK YANKEES
SPORT MAGAZINE '60 ALL-STAR SELECTION
MICKEY MANTLE Outfield/American League
ROGER MARIS
OUTFIELD
NEW YORK YANKEES
SPORT MAGAZINE '60 ALL-STAR SELECTION
ROGER MARIS Outfield/American League
GIL McDOUGALD
NEW YORK YANKEES 3rd BASE-2nd BASE
ZACK MONROE
PITCHER
NEW YORK YANKEES
BOBBY RICHARDSON
NEW YORK YANKEES SECOND BASE
BOBBY SHANTZ
PITCHER
NEW YORK YANKEES
SPORT MAGAZINE
1960 ROOKIE STAR
BILL SHORT N.Y. YANKEES • PITCHER
BILL SKOWRON
NEW YORK YANKEES FIRST BASE
SPORT MAGAZINE '60 ALL-STAR SELECTION
BILL SKOWRON 1st Base/American League
YANKEES
CASEY STENGEL
MANAGER • NEW YORK
RALPH TERRY
PITCHER
NEW YORK YANKEES
BOB TURLEY
PITCHER
NEW YORK YANKEES

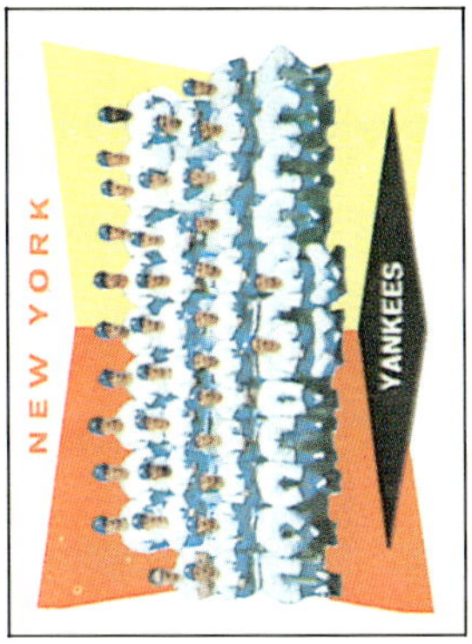

1961

With muscular assists from Roger Maris and Mickey Mantle, Ralph Houk proved Casey Stengel wasn't such a tough act to follow as he managed the Bombers to a pennant and World Series win in 1961. The expanded American League embraced a longer, 162-game schedule in which Maris, hitting 61 home runs, unseated the immortal Babe Ruth as the game's one-season home run king.

Maris erased Ruth's 1927 mark of 60 homers on the final day of the season with a solo shot at Yankee Stadium. For much of the summer Maris and Mantle captured the headlines with their long-distance slugging. But a hip injury sidelined Mantle in the final weeks and he finished with 54 homers as the club slammed a record 240. Maris, gaining his second straight MVP award, led the league with 142 RBIs.

Veteran southpaw Whitey Ford, the Cy Young winner, was 25-4. Ralph Terry won 16 and Bill Stafford 14, while rookie Rollie Sheldon contributed 11 victories. Luis Arroyo, relieving in 65 games, was 15-5. The Yankees then completed their blue-ribbon season by vanquishing the Cincinnati Reds in a five-game World Series.

1961
ROOKIE
FRITZ BRICKELL
Shortstop
New York
Yankees

BOB CERV
Outfield
New York
Yankees

JIM COATES
Pitcher
New York
Yankees

JOE DeMAESTRI
Infield
New York
Yankees

ART DITMAR
Pitcher
New York
Yankees

RYNE DUREN
Pitcher
New York
Yankees

WHITEY FORD
Pitcher
New York
Yankees

1960 WORLD SERIES
GAME #6
Ford Pitches Second Shutout

AMERICAN LEAGUE
Sporting News
ALL STAR
WHITEY FORD—PITCH. (L)

RALPH HOUK
Mgr. New York Yankees

ELSTON HOWARD
Catcher
New York
Yankees

1961
ROOKIE
DERON JOHNSON
Third Base-Outfield
New York
Yankees

TONY KUBEK
Shortstop
New York
Yankees

LARSEN PITCHES
PERFECT GAME

HECTOR LOPEZ
Outfield
New York
Yankees

DUKE MAAS
Pitcher
New York
Yankees

MICKEY MANTLE
Outfield
New York Yankees

MANTLE BLASTS 565 FT. HOME RUN

1960 WORLD SERIES
GAME #2
Mantle Slams 2 Homers

AMERICAN LEAGUE
Sporting News
ALL STAR
MICKEY MANTLE—CF

ROGER MARIS
Outfield
New York Yankees

AMERICAN LEAGUE
Sporting News
ALL STAR
ROGER MARIS—RF

DANNY McDEVITT
Pitcher
New York Yankees

BOBBY RICHARDSON
Second Base
New York Yankees

1960 WORLD SERIES
GAME #3
Richardson Is Hero

1961 ROOKIE
ROLAND SHELDON
Pitcher
New York Yankees

BILL SHORT
Pitcher
New York Yankees

BILL SKOWRON
First Base
New York Yankees

AMERICAN LEAGUE
Sporting News
ALL STAR
BILL SKOWRON—1B

BILL STAFFORD
Pitcher
New York Yankees

RALPH TERRY
Pitcher
New York Yankees

BOB TURLEY
Pitcher
New York Yankees

1962

It became two pennants and as many World Series wins for Ralph Houk and the Yankees in 1962. Though neither Mickey Mantle nor Roger Maris came close to duplicating their 1961 numbers, the Yankees began to roll in the second half of the season and won the pennant by five lengths over the Minnesota Twins.

Maris, under intense pressure from fans and media, finished with 33 homers and 100 RBIs. Mantle, again downed by injuries, hit 30 home runs and had 89 runs batted in, and was awarded the MVP for his efforts. Bobby Richardson and rookie Tom Tresh were big contributors, with Richardson batting .302 and Tresh earning the Rookie of the Year accolade with his .286 average plus 20 homers and 93 RBIs.

The pitching staff, not nearly as deep as many of its predecessors, was led by Ralph Terry's 23 wins. Whitey Ford won 17 and his 2.90 ERA was the third best in the league. Bill Stafford was 14-9 but Rollie Sheldon, 11-9 as a freshman in '61, fell to 7-8.

Houk and the Yankees then punctuated their season by defeating the San Francisco Giants in a World Series that went the full seven-game distance.

WORLD SERIES
FORD SETS NEW MARK

WHITEY
FORD
N. Y. YANKEES P

FORD TOSSES A CURVE

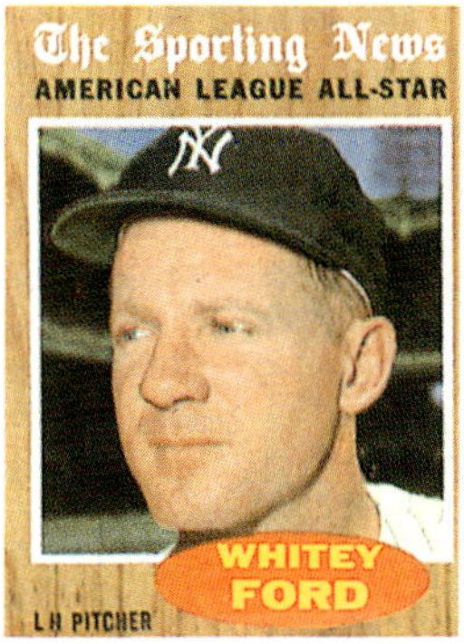
The Sporting News
AMERICAN LEAGUE ALL-STAR
WHITEY FORD
LH PITCHER

BILLY
GARDNER
N. Y. YANKEES 3B

1962 ROOKIE
JAKE
GIBBS
N. Y. YANKEES 3B

RALPH
HOUK
N. Y. YANKEES MGR

The Sporting News
AMERICAN LEAGUE ALL-STAR
ELSTON HOWARD
CATCHER

ELSTON
HOWARD
N. Y. YANKEES C

KUBEK MAKES THE DOUBLE PLAY

TONY
KUBEK
N. Y. YANKEES SS

HECTOR
LOPEZ
N. Y. YANKEES OF

MICKEY
MANTLE
N. Y. YANKEES OF

THE SWITCH HITTER CONNECTS

The Sporting News
AMERICAN LEAGUE ALL-STAR
MICKEY MANTLE
OUTFIELD

ROGER
MARIS
N. Y. YANKEES OF

MARIS WINS IT IN THE 9TH
WORLD SERIES

MARIS BLASTS 61ST

HAL
RENIFF
N. Y. YANKEES P

BOBBY
RICHARDSON
N. Y. YANKEES 2B

ROBIN
ROBERTS
N. Y. YANKEES P

ROLAND
SHELDON
N. Y. YANKEES P

BILL
SKOWRON

BILL
STAFFORD
N. Y. YANKEES P

1962 ROOKIE
HAL
STOWE
N. Y. YANKEES P

RALPH
TERRY
N. Y. YANKEES P

1962 ROOKIE
TOM
TRESH
N. Y. YANKEES SS

BOB
TURLEY
N. Y. YANKEES P

WORLD SERIES
FORD SETS NEW MARK

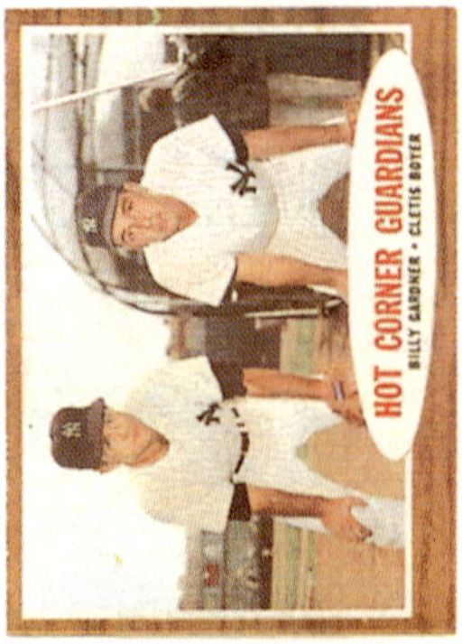
HOT CORNER GUARDIANS
BILLY GARDNER • CLETIS BOYER

NEW YORK YANKEES

WORLD SERIES
YANKS WIN OPENER

1963

The Yankees and manager Ralph Houk made it three-for-three in 1963, winning the pennant by 10½ games, the widest margin of victory in the American League since 1947 when the Yankees won by a dozen. This time, however, the vaunted Bombers failed to attach a World Series triumph, bowing in four straight to the pitching-rich Los Angeles Dodgers.

Despite Mickey Mantle's appearing in only 65 games because of a series of ailments, including a fractured left foot, the Yankees assumed command in mid-June and were never headed. Roger Maris, limited to 90 games because of assorted hurts, batted .269 with 23 homers and 53 RBIs. Mantle had 15 homers and just 35 runs batted in though batting .314. Elston Howard, the league's Most Valuable Player, gained that honor with a .287 average plus 28 homers and 85 RBIs. Newcomer Joe Pepitone hit .271 with 27 homers and led the club with 89 RBIs.

Whitey Ford, at 24-7, and sophomore righthander Jim Bouton, 21-7, were the team's top pitchers. Lefty Al Downing, 13-5, and the veteran Ralph Terry, 17-15, gave Houk some solid pitching performances.

CLETE
BOYER
N. Y. YANKEES 3B

HAL
BROWN
NEW YORK YANKEES P

TEX
CLEVENGER
NEW YORK YANKEES P

JIM
COATES
N. Y. YANKEES PITCHER

BUD
DALEY
N. Y. YANKEES PITCHER

WORLD
SERIES
GAME
#1
YANKS' FORD WINS
SERIES OPENER

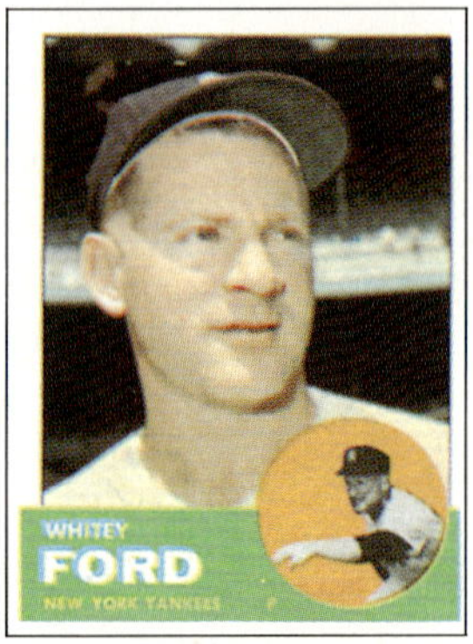
WHITEY
FORD
NEW YORK YANKEES P

RALPH
HOUK
NEW YORK YANKEES MGR.
Yankees

ELSTON
HOWARD
N. Y. YANKEES CATCHER

TONY
KUBEK
N. Y. YANKEES SS

BILL
KUNKEL
NEW YORK YANKEES P

PHIL
LINZ
N. Y. YANKEES INF.

DALE
LONG
NEW YORK YANKEES 1B

HECTOR
LOPEZ
N. Y. YANKEES OF

MICKEY
MANTLE
N. Y. YANKEES OF

ROGER
MARIS
NEW YORK YANKEES OF

WORLD SERIES GAME #3
MARIS SPARKS YANKEE RALLY

JOE
PEPITONE
NEW YORK YANKEES 1B

HAL
RENIFF
NEW YORK YANKEES P

BOBBY
RICHARDSON
NEW YORK YANKEES 2B

ROLAND
SHELDON
NEW YORK YANKEES P

BILL
STAFFORD
N. Y. YANKEES PITCHER

WORLD SERIES GAME #7
YANKS CELEBRATE AS TERRY WINS

RALPH
TERRY
N. Y. YANKEES P

WORLD SERIES GAME #5
TRESH'S HOMER DEFEATS GIANTS

TOPPS 1962 ALL-STAR ROOKIE
TOM
TRESH
NEW YORK YANKEES OF

STAN
WILLIAMS
N. Y. YANKEES PITCHER

BOMBERS' BEST
Tom Tresh • Mickey Mantle • Bobby Richardson

NEW YORK YANKEES

1964

The irrepressible Yogi Berra and the CBS broadcasting system dominated the Yankees' headlines in 1964. Berra, replacing Ralph Houk who became the general manager following the 1963 season, made it five straight flags for the Bombers.

In August, while the club was still struggling in the race, CBS paid $11.2 million for 80% of the stock held by longtime partners Dan Topping and Del Webb. The sale created a rhubarb among American League owners but it was overshadowed by the tight flag scramble.

On the next to last day of the season, Berra and the Yankees emerged one game over the Chicago White Sox. Mickey Mantle batted .303 and had 35 homers and 111 RBIs, while Roger Maris hit 26 homers and had 71 RBIs. Elston Howard, at .313, led the club in that regard.

The late-season acquisition of reliever Pete Ramos from Cleveland, plus the promotion of Mel Stottlemyre in August, bolstered the pitching staff. Whitey Ford was 17-6, Jim Bouton 18-13 and Al Downing 13-8. Stottlemyre, in 12 starts, was 9-3 with a 2.06 ERA.

Following the World Series, which the Yankees lost to the St. Louis Cardinals in seven games, the baseball world was stunned when the Yankees fired Berra as manager and replaced him with his Series conqueror, Johnny Keane.

YANKEES
STEVE HAMILTON pitcher

YANKEES
ELSTON HOWARD catcher

YANKEES
TONY KUBEK shortstop

YANKEES
PHIL LINZ inf-of

YANKEES
HECTOR LOPEZ outfield

YANKEES
MICKEY MANTLE outfield

YANKEES
ROGER MARIS outfielder

YANKEES
JOE PEPITONE 1st base

YANKEES
HAL RENIFF pitcher

YANKEES
BOBBY RICHARDSON 2b

YANKEES
BILL STAFFORD pitcher

YANKEES
RALPH TERRY pitcher

YANKEES
TOM TRESH outfield

YANKEES
STAN WILLIAMS pitcher

YOUNG ACES
AL DOWNING • JIM BOUTON

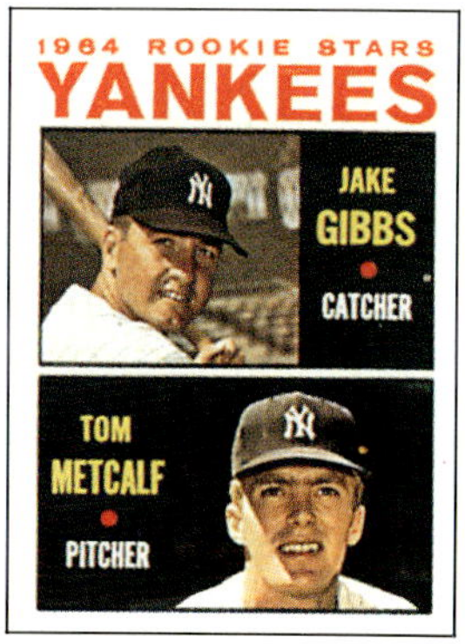
1964 ROOKIE STARS
YANKEES
JAKE GIBBS
CATCHER
TOM METCALF
PITCHER

1965

The Yankees, after winning 14 pennants and nine World Series in the preceding 16 years, began learning how the other half live when they tumbled to a horrendous sixth place finish in 1965.

Johnny Keane's debut as Yankees' skipper was a sad one as his club finished 25 games behind the flag-winning Minnesota Twins in what became the Bombers' worst windup in 40 years.

Injuries, of course, contributed to the downfall, with Mickey Mantle, Elston Howard, Roger Maris, Tony Kubeck and Bill Stafford among the major casualties. Mantle batted .255 with 19 homers, while Roger Maris, in just 46 games, hit .239 with eight four-baggers. Kubeck hit .218 and Howard .233 with nine homers.

Stafford, bothered by tendinitis, was 3-8 and Jim Bouton went from 18 victories in 1964 to four in '65. Mel Stottlemyre and Whitey Ford gave Keane quality pitching. Stottlemyre finished at 20-9 and Ford, coming off shoulder surgery, produced a 16-13 mark.

YANKEES
OUTFIELD
DUKE CARMEL

YANKEES
PITCHER
AL DOWNING

YANKEES
PITCHER
WHITEY FORD

YANKEES
INFIELD-OF
PEDRO GONZALEZ

YANKEES
PITCHER
STEVE HAMILTON

YANKEES
CATCHER
ELSTON HOWARD

YANKEES
MANAGER
JOHNNY KEA

YANKEES
SHORTSTOP
TONY KUBEK

YANKEES
INF-OUTFIELD
PHIL LINZ

YANKEES
OUTFIELD
HECTOR LOPEZ

MANTLE'S CLUTCH HR
GAME #3 NEW YORK 2 ST. LOUIS 1
WORLD SERIES

YANKEES
OUTFIELD
MICKEY MANTLE

YANKEES
OUTFIELD
ROGER MARIS

YANKEES
PITCHER
PETE MIKKELSEN

YANKEES
1st BASE
JOE PEPITONE

YANKEES
PITCHER
PEDRO RAMOS

YANKEES
PITCHER
HAL RENIFF

YANKEES
2nd BASE
BOBBY RICHARDSON

YANKEES
CATCHER
BOB SCHMIDT

YANKEES
PITCHER
ROLAND SHELDON

YANKEES
PITCHER
BILL STAFFORD

STOTTLEMYRE WINS
WORLD SERIES

YANKEES
PITCHER
MEL STOTTLEMYRE

YANKEES
OUTFIELD
TOM TRESH

1965 ROOKIE STARS
JAKE GIBBS catcher
ELVIO JIMENEZ outfield
YANKEES

YANKEES
1965 ROOKIE STARS
GIL BLANCO PITCHER
ART LOPEZ
ROSS MOSCHITTO

YANKEES
1ST PLACE • AMERICAN LEAGUE

1966

If the Yankees thought 1965 was a nightmare, then words don't describe their 1966 efforts. Johnny Keane was fired as manager in May, but even Ralph Houk's return as skipper couldn't prevent the club from experiencing its first cellar windup since 1912.

The team wound up 19 games below .500 and 26½ lengths behind the pennant-winning Baltimore Orioles. Virtually all 1966 numbers posted by the Yankees were negatives as they lost 38 one-run games and hit a mere .235 as a unit.

Mickey Mantle, on fragile legs, hit .288 and had 23 home runs. Roger Maris, who was dealt to St. Louis in December 1965, ended his Yankees' career with 13 homers and a .233 average. Joe Pepitone, despite a .255 average, was a bright spot with 31 homers and 83 RBIs.

As for the pitching, no hurler won more than 12 and that was newcomer Fritz Peterson at 12-11. Mel Stottlemyre went from 20-9 to 12-20. Al Downing was 10-11 and Whitey Ford, who underwent surgery in September, ended at 2-5.

YANKEES
BOB FRIEND pitcher

YANKEES
JAKE GIBBS catcher

YANKEES
STEVE HAMILTON pitcher

YANKEES
ELSTON HOWARD catcher

YANKEES
JOHNNY KEANE manager

YANKEES
HECTOR LOPEZ outfield

YANKEES
MICKEY MANTLE outfield

YANKEES
ROGER MARIS outfield

YANKEES
JOE PEPITONE 1st base

YANKEES
PEDRO RAMOS pitcher

YANKEES
HAL RENIFF pitcher

YANKEES
ROGER REPOZ outfield

YANKEES
BOBBY RICHARDSON 2b

YANKEES
MEL STOTTLEMYRE pitcher

YANKEES
TOM TRESH outfield

1966 ROOKIE STARS
YANKEES
ROY WHITE 2b-of
RICH BECK pitcher

1967

The Yankees managed to avert a second straight cellar finish when they landed ninth, 20 games behind the flag-winning Boston Red Sox in 1967. A porous defense and a feeble offense virtually doomed the Yankees from the outset.

Horace Clarke, at .272, had the highest batting average, while Tom Tresh, rookie Bill Robinson and Joe Pepitone had disappointing seasons. Pepitone's home run output dipped from 31 to 13, while Tresh batted .219 and Robinson a feeble .196.

Mel Stottlemyre, at 15-15 was the club's top winning pitcher. Al Downing followed with a 14-10 log. Fritz Peterson finished at 8-14 and Whitey Ford, plagued by assorted arm miseries, retired from active competition on May 31.

HORACE CLARKE • 2B
YANKEES

LOU CLINTON • OUTFIELD
YANKEES

AL DOWNING • PITCHER
YANKEES

WHITEY FORD PITCHER
YANKEES

JAKE GIBBS • CATCHER
YANKEES

STEVE HAMILTON • P
YANKEES

RALPH HOUK • MGR.
YANKEES

ELSTON HOWARD CATCHER
YANKEES

DICK HOWSER • SS
YANKEES

MICKEY MANTLE • OF
YANKEES

JOE PEPITONE • 1B-OF
YANKEES

FRITZ PETERSON • P
YANKEES

HAL RENIFF • PITCHER
YANKEES

CHARLEY SMITH • 3B
YANKEES

MEL STOTTLEMYRE • P
YANKEES

FRED TALBOT • PITCHER
YANKEES

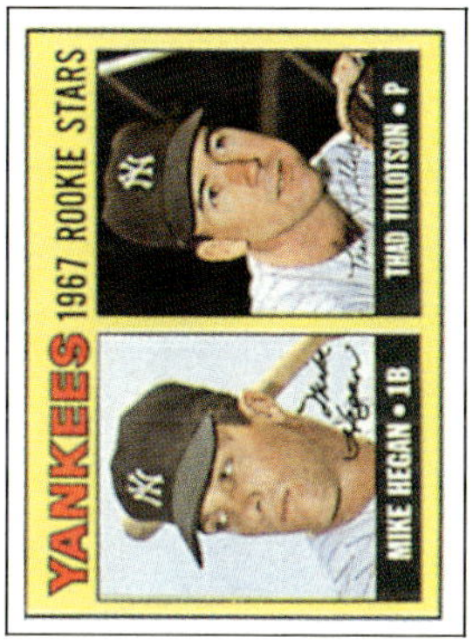

1968

The Yankees, despite a team batting average of .214, continued their slow march to respectability when they finished fifth in 1968. Roy White, at .267, was the club's top hitter and Mickey Mantle, playing 131 games at first base, contributed 18 home runs to raise his career total to 536, third on the all-time list. Before the 1969 season opened, Mantle announced his retirement.

It was pitching that kept the Yankees afloat as the staff posted a composite 2.79 earned run average. Mel Stottlemyre (21-12) and freshman Stan Bahnsen (17-12) were the club's big winners. Fritz Peterson produced a 12-11 record.

Lindy McDaniel, acquired from San Francisco in July, moved into the bullpen and gave the Yankees effective relief help the rest of the way. In 24 appearances the righthander won four of five decisions and saved another 10 games.

RUBEN
AMARO
SHORTSTOP
YANKEES

STEVE
BARBER
PITCHER
YANKEES

JIM
BOUTON
PITCHER
YANKEES

HORACE
CLARKE
2nd BASE
YANKEES

AL
DOWNING
PITCHER
YANKEES

JAKE
GIBBS
CATCHER
YANKEES

STEVE
HAMILTON
PITCHER
YANKEES

MIKE
HEGAN
1B-OF
YANKEES

RALPH
HOUK
MANAGER
YANKEES

DICK
HOWSER
SS-3B
YANKEES

ANDY
KOSCO
OUTFIELD
YANKEES

MICKEY
MANTLE
1st BASE
YANKEES

GENE
MICHAEL
SHORTSTOP
YANKEES

BILL
MONBOUQUETTE
PITCHER
YANKEES

JOE
PEPITONE
OUTFIELD
YANKEES

FRITZ
PETERSON
PITCHER
YANKEES

OUTFIELD
YANKEES
BILL
ROBINSON

3rd BASE
YANKEES
CHARLIE
SMITH

PITCHER
YANKEES
MEL
STOTTLEMYRE

PITCHER
YANKEES
FRED
TALBOT

OUTFIELD
YANKEES
TOM
TRESH

PITCHER
YANKEES
JOE
VERBANIC

OUTFIELD
YANKEES
STEVE
WHITAKER

OUTFIELD
YANKEES
ROY
WHITE

PITCHER
YANKEES
DOOLEY
WOMACK

1968 ROOKIE STARS
FRANK FERNANDEZ • C
STAN BAHNSEN • P
YANKEES

1969

It was the year baseball adopted the two-division setup, but the best the virtually starless Yankees could do was fifth place in the six-club American League East in 1969.

Mickey Mantle was gone and the offense produced a mere .235 batting average. Roy White's .290 was the best among the regulars, while Joe Pepitone led in homers with 27 and Bobby Murcer, with 26 homers, paced the club in RBIs with 82.

Again it was the pitching, though spotty at times, that helped the Yankees finish one game below .500. Mel Stottlemyre was tops with a 20-14 mark and Fritz Peterson followed at 17-16. Stan Bahnsen, the league's top rookie in 1968, encountered the feared sophomore jinx and dipped from 17-12 to 9-16. The relievers, with such as Lindy McDaniel and Steve Hamilton contributing, got an additional boost when Jack Aker came over from Oakland in May and posted eight wins and 11 saves.

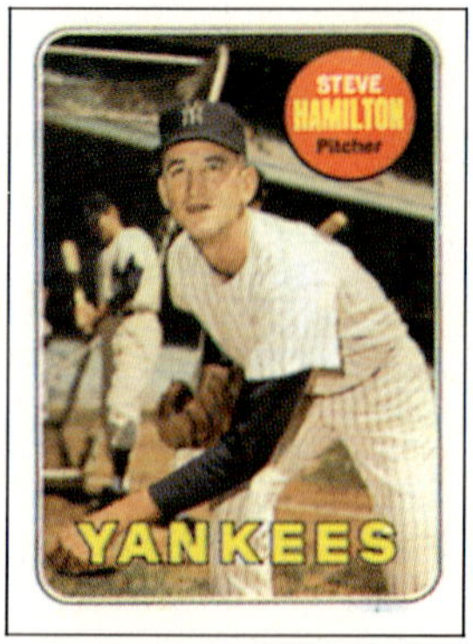

RALPH
HOUK
Manager
YANKEES

MIKE
KEKICH
Pitcher
YANKEES

MICKEY
MANTLE
1st Base
YANKEES

LINDY
McDANIEL
Pitcher
YANKEES

GENE
MICHAEL
Shortstop
YANKEES

BOBBY
MURCER
3rd Base
YANKEES

NATE
OLIVER
2nd Base
YANKEES

JOE
PEPITONE
1st Base
YANKEES

FRITZ
PETERSON
Pitcher
YANKEES

BILL
ROBINSON
Outfield
YANKEES

DICK
SIMPSON
Outfield
YANKEES

MEL
STOTTLEMYRE
Pitcher
YANKEES

FRED
TALBOT
Pitcher
YANKEES

TOM
TRESH
SS-OF
YANKEES

JOE
VERBANIC
Pitcher
YANKEES

ROY
WHITE
Outfield
YANKEES

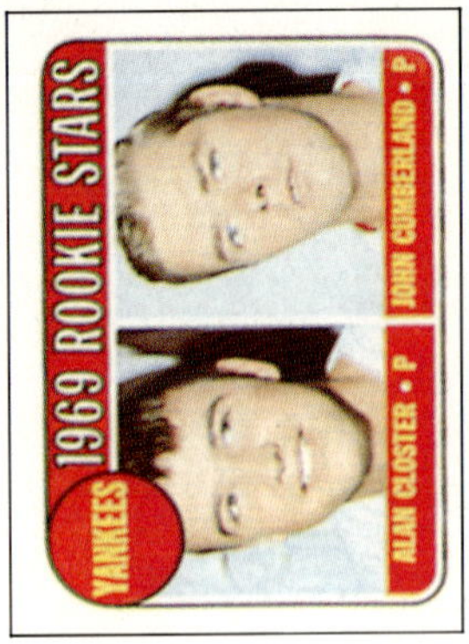

1970

What was to become a turbulent decade in the club's long history opened with the Yankees finishing a surprising second in the American League's Eastern Division in 1970.

Ralph Houk was named Manager of the Year, despite his club finishing 15 lengths behind the champion Orioles. Thurman Munson, a .302-hitting catcher, was Rookie of the Year and Danny Cater batted .301. Roy White, at .296, hit 22 homers and produced 94 runs batted in.

Longtime pitching ace Mel Stottlemyre, a victim of poor mound luck, won 15 and lost 13, while Fritz Peterson won 20 and dropped 13. Stan Bahnsen was 14-11. If there was a pitching problem it was the failure to find a consistent fourth and fifth starter.

The bullpen was a Yankees plus. Lindy McDaniel won nine and saved 29 others and Jack Aker, despite back troubles in the second half, had four wins and 16 rescues.

YANKEES
Danny Cater
1ST BASE

YANKS
Horace Clarke
2ND BASE

YANKS
Frank Fernandez
C-OF

YANKS
Jake Gibbs
CATCHER

YANKEES
Steve Hamilton
PITCHER

YANKS
Ralph Houk
MANAGER

YANKEES
Mike Kekich
PITCHER

YANKEES
Jerry Kenney
3RD BASE

YANKS
Lindy McDaniel
PITCHER

YANKEES
Gene Michael
SHORTSTOP

YANKS
Bobby Murcer
OUTFIELD

YANKEES
Fritz Peterson
PITCHER

YANKEES
Bill Robinson
OUTFIELD

YANKEES
Mel Stottlemyre
PITCHER

YANKS
Frank Tepedino
OUTFIELD

YANKEES
Joe Verbanic
PITCHER

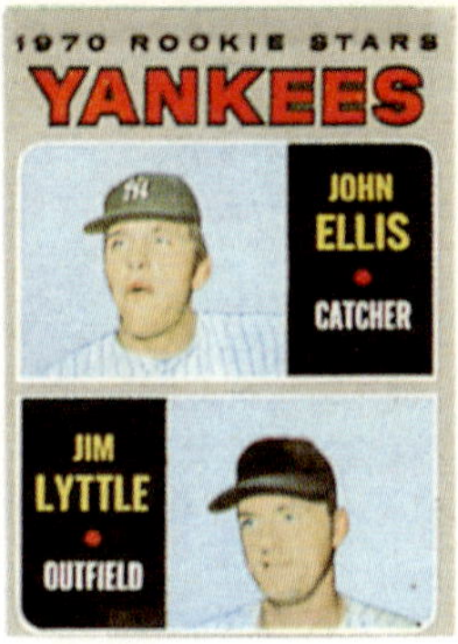

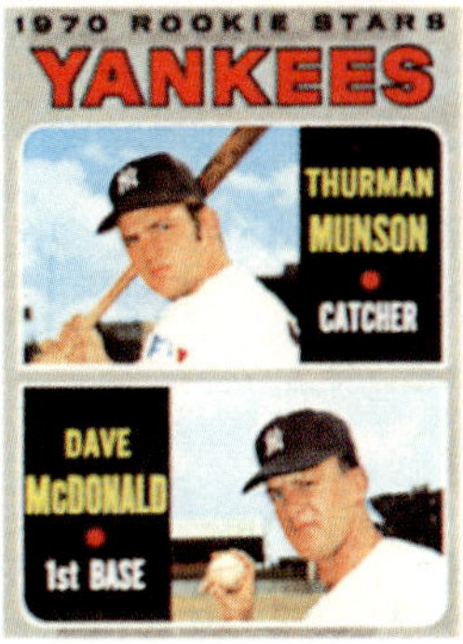

1971

The 1971 season, which began for the Yankees on an optimistic note, ended on a sour one as the club, beset by defensive and bullpen troubles, toppled from second to fourth place.

Bobby Mercer's .331 average was a plus. Ditto Roy White's .292 and the 84 RBIs he added to the attack. Veteran Felipe Alou, acquired from Oakland in April, had a hot second half and finished with .288 and 69 runs batted in.

Mel Stottlemyre, with 16 wins, and Fritz Peterson, with 15, led the pitching staff. Stan Bahnsen was 14-12 and young Steve Kline 12-13. The relief corps, however, was unproductive. The 'pen, so helpful in 1970, had a total of a dozen saves with the advertised aces, Lindy McDaniel and Jack Aker, notching just four apiece.

YANKEES
jack aker • pitcher

YANKEES
stan bahnsen • pitcher

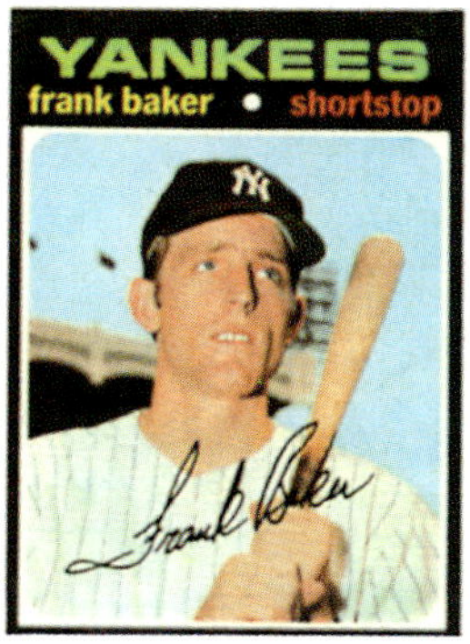
YANKEES
frank baker • shortstop

YANKEES
curt blefary • 1b-of

YANKEES
bill burbach • pitcher

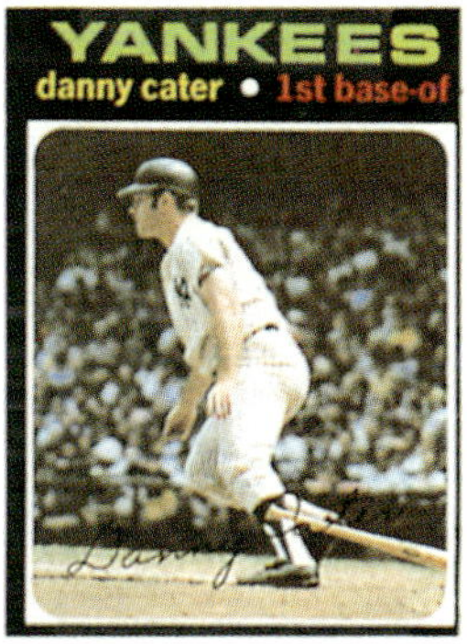
YANKEES
danny cater • 1st base-of

YANKEES
horace clarke • 2nd base

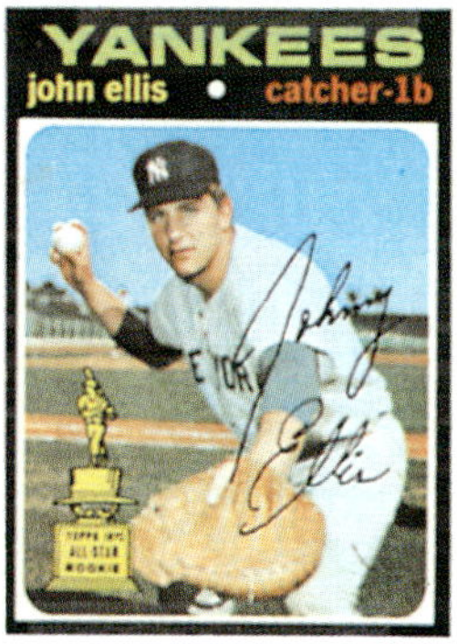
YANKEES
john ellis • catcher-1b

YANKEES
rob gardner • pitcher

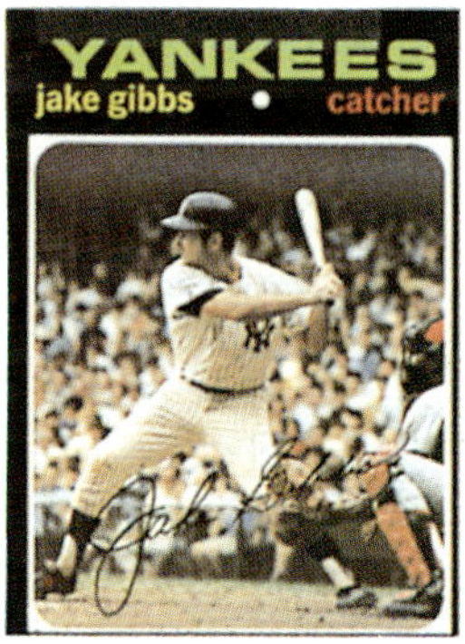
YANKEES
jake gibbs • catcher

YANKEES
ron hansen • infield

YANKEES
ralph houk • manager

YANKEES
mike kekich • pitcher

YANKEES
jerry kenney • 3rd base

YANKEES
ron klimkowski • pitcher

YANKEES
steve kline • pitcher

YANKEES
jim lyttle • outfield

YANKEES
mike mc cormick • p

YANKEES
lindy mc daniel • pitcher

YANKEES
gene michael • shortstop

YANKEES
thurman munson • c

YANKEES
bobby murcer • outfield

YANKEES
fritz peterson • pitcher

YANKEES
mel stottlemyre • pitcher

YANKEES
frank tepedino • outfield

YANKEES
pete ward • 1b-of

YANKEES
gary waslewski • pitcher

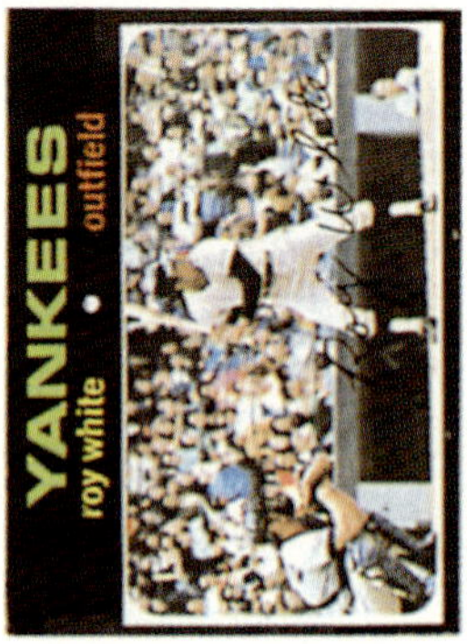
YANKEES
roy white • outfield

YANKEES
ron woods • outfield

1971 ROOKIE STARS
YANKEES
loyd colson
•
pitcher
bobby mitchell
•
outfield

YANKEES

1972

Another fourth-place finish was the Yankees' lot in 1972, but this time it wasn't the bullpen that was the cause. A spring training trade that netted Sparky Lyle from Boston paid dividends when the lefty won nine and saved a league-high 35.

A sputtering offense and inconsistent performances from the starters caused the Yankees' troubles. Bobby Murcer, after a woeful start, finished with 33 homers, 96 RBIs and a .292 average. Roy White hit only 10 homers and his .270 average was a 22-point dip from 1971.

Fritz Peterson won 17 and lost 15, while Mel Stottlemyre, experiencing a six-week dry spell, ended at 14-18. Steve Kline was 16-9 and Mike Kekich 10-13. Shortly after the season, the Yankees, in multi-player trades, obtained third baseman Graig Nettles from Cleveland and outfielder Matty Alou from Oakland.

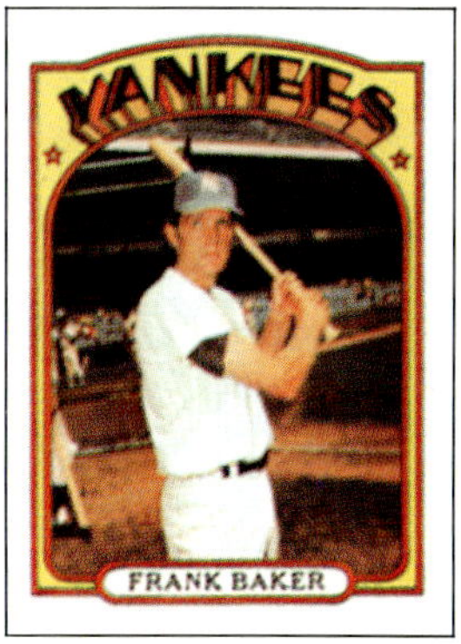

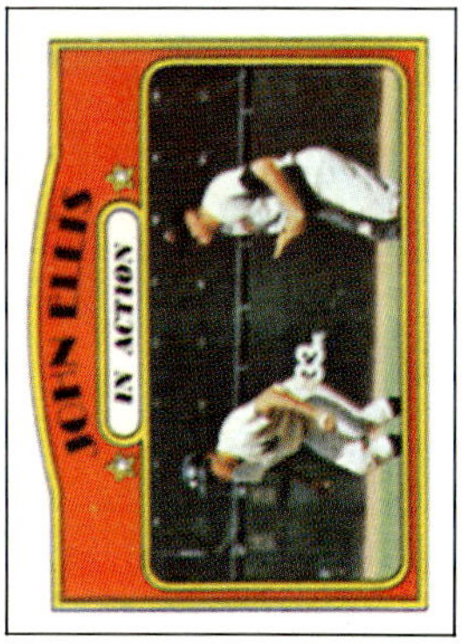

YANKEES
ROB GARDNER

YANKEES
JIM HARDIN

YANKEES
RALPH HOUK

YANKEES
MIKE KEKICH

YANKEES
JERRY KENNEY

YANKEES
STEVE KLINE

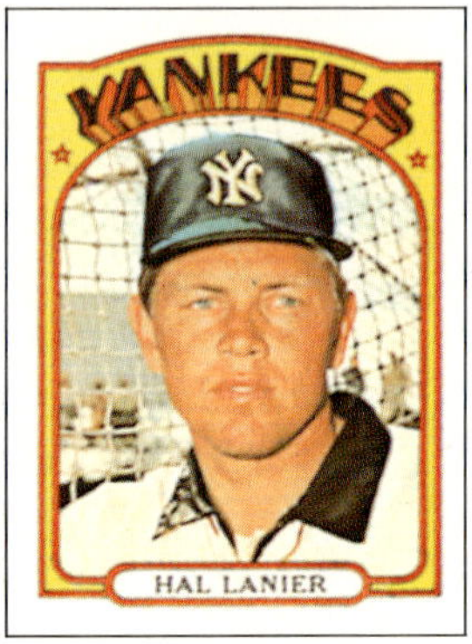
YANKEES
HAL LANIER

YANKEES
JIM MAGNUSON

YANKEES
LINDY McDANIEL

YANKEES
RICH McKINNEY

YANKEES
GENE MICHAEL

GENE MICHAEL
IN ACTION

YANKEES
THURMAN MUNSON

THURMAN MUNSON
IN ACTION

YANKEES
BOBBY MURCER

BOBBY MURCER
IN ACTION

YANKEES
FRITZ PETERSON

FRITZ PETERSON
IN ACTION

YANKEES
MEL STOTTLEMYRE

BOYHOOD PHOTOS
OF THE STARS
MEL STOTTLEMYRE

YANKEES
RON SWOBODA

YANKEES
GARY WASLEWSKI

YANKEES
ROY WHITE

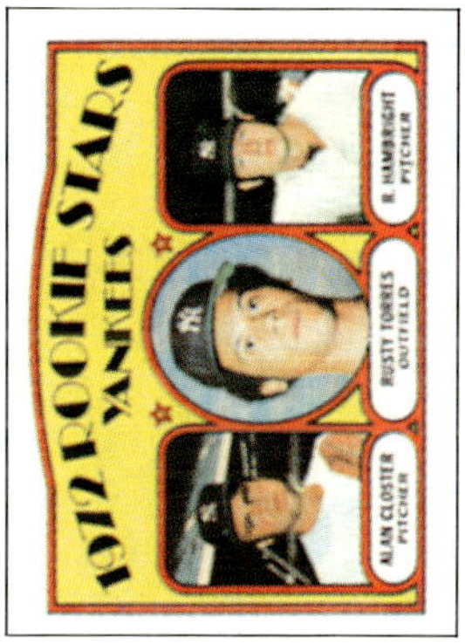
1972 ROOKIE STARS
YANKEES
ALAN CLOSTER
PITCHER
RUSTY TORRES
OUTFIELD
R. HAMBRIGHT
PITCHER

YANKEES

1973

The season didn't officially begin until April, but the Yankees made things happen in January when the CBS broadcasting system, in a surprise move, sold the club to a list of investors headed by Cleveland shipbuilder George M Steinbrenner 3d. Though listed as the general partner, Steinbrenner, saying he'd remain in the background, began casting a giant shadow early.

Another fourth-place finish was pretty much overlooked as manager Ralph Houk and general manager Lee MacPhail resigned when the season ended. Newcomers Graig Nettles and Matty Alou did their advertised thing. Alou, a contact hitter, batted .296, while Nettles, a powerman, hit 22 homers, had 81 RBIs and provided superior defense at third base. Thurman Munson added 20 homers, 74 RBIs and a .301 batting average.

Rookie righthander George (Doc) Medich broke in with a 14-9 record and a 2.95 earned run average. The veteran Mel Stottlemyre was 16-16. Fritz Peterson, who'd gotten the club unwanted publicity with the springtime announcement he and fellow lefty Mike Kekich had swapped wives and families, was 8-15. Kekich was traded to Cleveland in June.

CASEY
COX
NEW YORK YANKEES
PITCHER

COACHES
JIM HEGAN
ELSTON HOWARD
DICK HOWSER
JIM TURNER
RALPH
HOUK
NEW YORK YANKEES
MANAGER

MIKE
KEKICH
NEW YORK YANKEES
PITCHER

STEVE
KLINE
NEW YORK YANKEES
PITCHER

HAL
LANIER
NEW YORK YANKEES
3rd BASE

SPARKY
LYLE
NEW YORK YANKEES
PITCHER

LINDY
McDANIEL
NEW YORK YANKEES
PITCHER

SHORTSTOP
GENE
MICHAEL
NEW YORK YANKEES

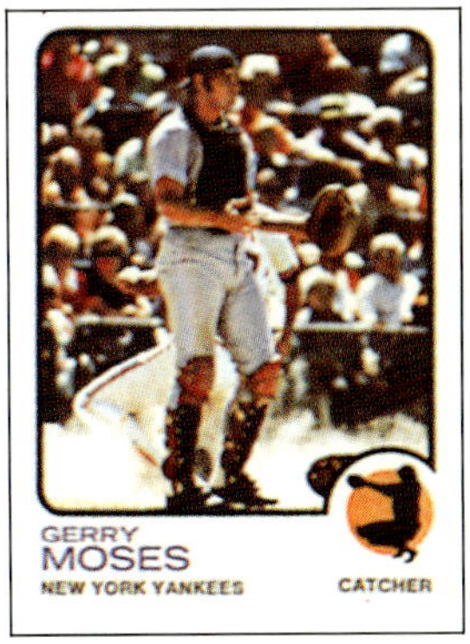
GERRY
MOSES
NEW YORK YANKEES
CATCHER

THURMAN
MUNSON
NEW YORK YANKEES
CATCHER

Boyhood Photos of the Stars
BOBBY
MURCER

BOBBY
MURCER
NEW YORK YANKEES
OUTFIELD

GRAIG
NETTLES
NEW YORK YANKEES
3rd BASE

FRITZ
PETERSON
NEW YORK YANKEES
PITCHER

CELERINO
SANCHEZ
NEW YORK YANKEES
3rd BASE

MEL
STOTTLEMYRE
NEW YORK YANKEES
PITCHER

1974

With historic Yankee Stadium undergoing much needed repairs, the club moved to Shea Stadium in April 1974 to begin a two season residency as tenants of the rival New York Mets.

The change of venue, though not popular with the Yankees, did result in a second-place finish, two games behind the division champion Baltimore Orioles.

Former Pittsburgh skipper Bill Virdon became the club's no-nonsense skipper and won himself Manager of the Year honors. Veteran front-office operator Gabe Paul, a member of George Steinbrenner's hierarchy, swung some deals that enabled the club to advance.

Such newcomers as Lou Piniella (.305) and Elliott Maddox (.303) plus holdover Ron Blomberg (.311) aided considerably. Ditto Graig Nettles who hit 22 homers. Virdon's mid-season decision to move Maddox to centerfield and Bobby Murcer to right aided the defense.

Pat Dobson and Doc Medich each won 19 games and the sore-shouldered Mel Stottlemyre finished his career at 6-7. The bull of the pen was Sparky Lyle. He won nine, saved 15 and pitched to a 1.66 ERA.

NEW YORK
PITCHER
PAT DOBSON
YANKEES

NEW YORK
PITCHER
WAYNE GRANGER
YANKEES

NEW YORK
DES. HITTER
JIM RAY HART
YANKEES

NEW YORK
1st BASE
MIKE HEGAN
YANKEES

NEW YORK
PITCHER
STEVE KLINE
YANKEES

NEW YORK
INFIELD
HAL LANIER
YANKEES

NEW YORK
PITCHER
SPARKY LYLE
YANKEES

JIM MASON
SHORTSTOP
TRADED
TO NEW YORK YANKEES

NEW YORK
PITCHER
LINDY McDANIEL
YANKEES

NEW YORK
PITCHER
SAM McDOWELL
YANKEES

NEW YORK
PITCHER
42
GEORGE MEDICH
YANKEES

NEW YORK
SHORTSTOP
GENE MICHAEL
YANKEES

NEW YORK
CATCHER
NEW YORK
GERRY MOSES
YANKEES

NEW YORK
CATCHER
THURMAN MUNSON
YANKEES

NEW YORK
OUTFIELD
BOBBY MURCER
YANKEES

NEW YORK
3rd BASE
GRAIG NETTLES
YANKEES

NEW YORK
PITCHER
FRITZ
PETERSON
YANKEES

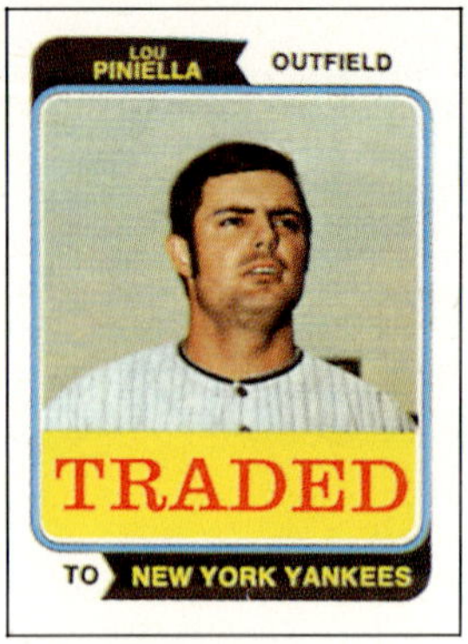
LOU
PINIELLA
OUTFIELD
TRADED
TO NEW YORK YANKEES

NEW YORK
3B-OF
CELERINO
SANCHEZ
YANKEES

NEW YORK
CATCHER
DUKE
SIMS
YANKEES

NEW YORK
2nd BASE
FRED
STANLEY
YANKEES

NEW YORK
PITCHER
MEL
STOTTLEMYRE
YANKEES

BILL
SUDAKIS
1B-OF
TRADED
TO NEW YORK YANKEES

NEW YORK
OUTFIELD
ROY
WHITE
YANKEES

NEW YORK YANKEES

1975

Catfish Hunter, Bobby Bonds and Billy Martin were among the new arrivals at Shea Stadium in 1975, but a third-place windup was the best the Yankees could do. Mishaps to Bonds, Elliott Maddox, Ron Blomberg and Lou Piniella offset Hunter's pitching and Thurman Munson's .318 batting average and 102 RBIs.

Hunter, a free agent from Oakland, signed a five-year deal worth $3.2 million and won 23 games. However, Doc Medich (16-16) and Pat Dobson (11-14) couldn't regain their 1974 form and the Bombers' bullpen could effect only 20 saves.

Bonds, obtained from the Giants for the popular Bobby Murcer, hit 32 homers and had 85 RBIs, but the leg injury he suffered in June restricted him the remainder of the season. Maddox, hitting .307 at the time, tore a knee cartilage shortly after Bonds went down and missed the rest of the race. A shoulder problem stopped Blomberg and an ear infection had Piniella in and out of the lineup.

In a surprise move, with the Yankees two games over .500 in August, Bill Virdon was dismissed and Martin hired but he was unable to challenge the front-running Red Sox.

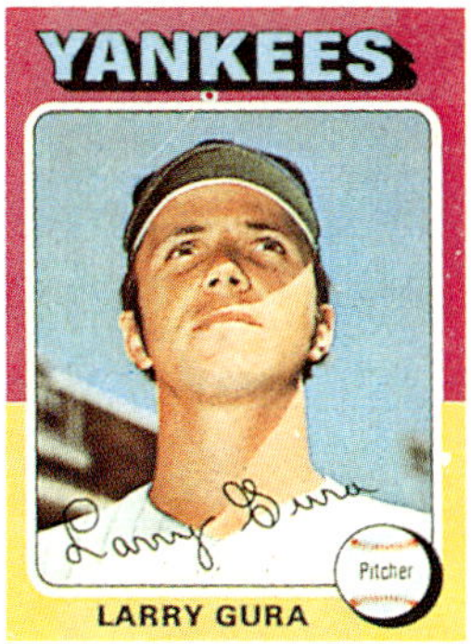

YANKEES
Pitcher
SPARKY LYLE

YANKEES
Outfield
ELLIOTT MADDOX

YANKEES
Shortstop
JIM MASON

YANKEES
Pitcher
RUDY MAY

YANKEES
Pitcher
GEORGE MEDICH

YANKEES
SS-2B
GENE MICHAEL

YANKEES
Catcher
THURMAN MUNSON

YANKEES
3rd Base
GRAIG NETTLES

YANKEES
Pitcher
DAVE PAGAN

YANKEES
Outfield
LOU PINIELLA

YANKEES
Infield
FRED STANLEY

YANKEES
Pitcher
MEL STOTTLEMYRE

YANKEES
DH-1B
BILL SUDAKIS

YANKEES
Pitcher
DICK TIDROW

YANKEES
Pitcher
CECIL UPSHAW

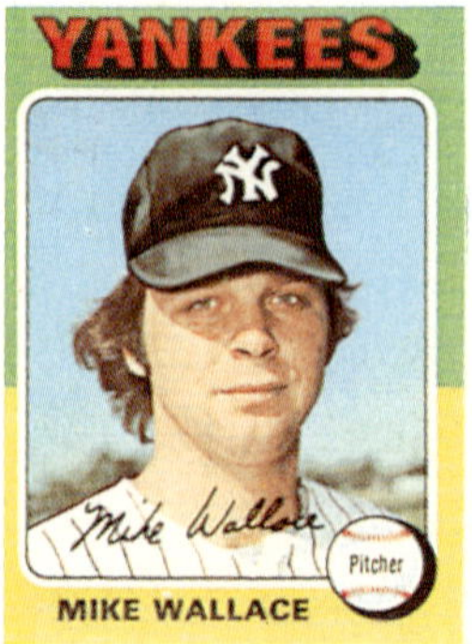
YANKEES
Pitcher
MIKE WALLACE

1976

The return to newly renovated Yankee Stadium in 1976 resulted in the Bombers winning a pennant for the first time since 1964. They won by 10½ games and defeated Kansas City in the playoffs on Chris Chambliss' sudden-death home run. Their dream of a world championship vanished, however, when they were swept four straight by Cincinnati in the Series.

Thurman Munson (.302) was the MVP and Graig Nettles' 32 home runs made him the league leader. Mickey Rivers, acquired from the Angels for Bobby Bonds, batted .312 and stole 43 bases. Ed Figueroa, who accompanied Rivers in the trade, won 19 games. Catfish Hunter had 17 wins, while Dock Ellis, traded from the Pirates, was 17-8.

The Yankees' staff had a league-leading 3.19 ERA. Sparky Lyle had 23 saves and righthander Dick Tidrow 10. On June 15 the Yankees ostensibly purchased Vida Blue from Oakland for $1.5 million, but the deal was canceled by Commissioner Bowie Kuhn.

DEC. 11 SPORTS EXTRA 1975
KEN BRETT TRADED TO YANKEES
PITCHER
KEN BRETT

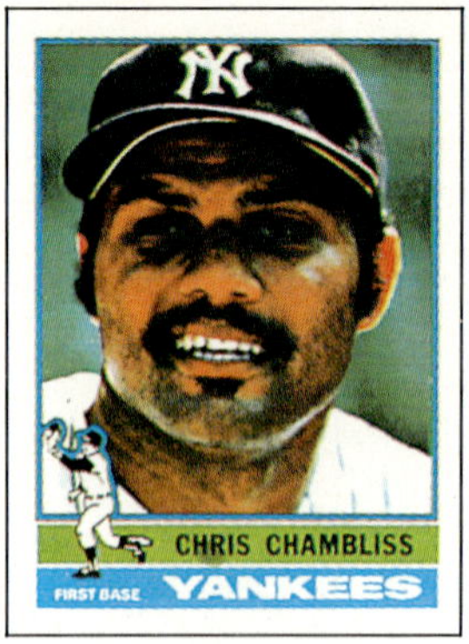
CHRIS CHAMBLISS
FIRST BASE
YANKEES

RICH COGGINS
OUTFIELD
YANKEES

RICK DEMPSEY
CATCHER
YANKEES

PAT DOBSON
PITCHER
YANKEES

DEC. 11 SPORTS EXTRA 1975
YANKEES GET DOCK ELLIS FROM BUCS
PITCHER
DOCK ELLIS

DEC. 11 SPORTS EXTRA 1975
FIGUEROA COMES TO YANKEES IN SWAP
PITCHER
ED FIGUEROA

NOV. 22 SPORTS EXTRA 1975
YANKEES TAKE GAMBLE ON OSCAR
OUTFIELD
OSCAR GAMBLE

LARRY GURA
PITCHER
YANKEES

ED HERRMANN
CATCHER
YANKEES

JIM HUNTER
PITCHER
YANKEES

SPARKY LYLE
PITCHER
YANKEES

ELLIOTT MADDOX
OUTFIELD
YANKEES

TIPPY MARTINEZ
PITCHER
YANKEES

RUDY MAY
PITCHER
YANKEES

GEORGE MEDICH
PITCHER
YANKEES

AL ALL STAR Catcher
THURMAN MUNSON
YANKEES

AL ALL STAR 3rd Base
GRAIG NETTLES
YANKEES

LOU PINIELLA
OUTFIELD
YANKEES

DEC. 11 SPORTS EXTRA 1975
BRONX BOMBERS GET WILLIE RANDOLPH
SECOND BASE
WILLIE RANDOLPH

DEC. 11 SPORTS EXTRA 1975
MICK THE QUICK TRADED TO YANKEES
OUTFIELD
MICKEY RIVERS

FRED STANLEY
SHORTSTOP
YANKEES

DICK TIDROW
PITCHER
YANKEES

ROY WHITE
OUTFIELD
YANKEES

WALT WILLIAMS
OUTFIELD
YANKEES

MGR. BILLY MARTIN
NEW YORK YANKEES

1977

The five-year, $2.96-million contract that free agent Reggie Jackson signed with the Yankees reverberated throughout the 1977 season, which ended with them winning the flag and defeating the Dodgers in a World Series in which Jackson was the catalyst.

Jackson, who hit 32 homers and drove in 110 runs, collided several times with manager Billy Martin in a battle of personalities during the hectic summer. The most famous was their near fistfight in the dugout during a TV game at Boston in June. Jackson, however, captured the headlines when he hit five homers in the Series, including a record-tying three in the final game.

The pennant, won by 2½ lengths over Boston, was made possible by, in addition to Jackson, Mickey Rivers' .326 batting average, the .308 that helped Thurman Munson be the MVP, Lou Piniella's .330 and Graig Nettles' 37 homers and 107 RBIs.

Ron Guidry (16-7), Ed Figueroa (16-11), Don Gullett (14-4) and Mike Torrez (17-13) paced the mound staff. But it was longtime reliever Sparky Lyle who captured the Cy Young Award with 13 wins and 26 saves.

YANKEES
CATCHER
FRAN HEALY

YANKEES
PITCHER
KEN HOLTZMAN

YANKEES
PITCHER
JIM HUNTER

YANKEES
OUTFIELD
REGGIE JACKSON

YANKEES
PITCHER
SPARKY LYLE

YANKEES
OUTFIELD
ELLIOTT MADDOX

YANKEES
DES. HITTER
CARLOS MAY

YANKEES
CATCHER
THURMAN MUNSON
A.L. ALL-STARS

YANKEES
3rd BASE
GRAIG NETTLES

YANKEES
OUTFIELD
LOU PINIELLA

YANKEES
2nd BASE
WILLIE RANDOLPH

YANKEES
OUTFIELD
MICKEY RIVERS

YANKEES
SHORTSTOP
FRED STANLEY

YANKEES
PITCHER
DICK TIDROW

YANKEES
OUTFIELD
CESAR TOVAR

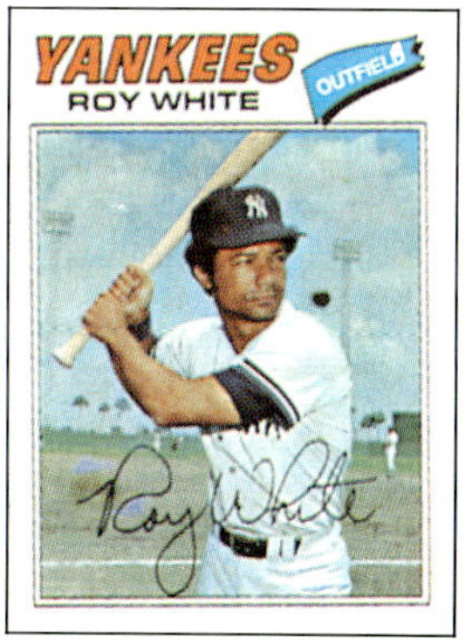
YANKEES
OUTFIELD
ROY WHITE

1978

A fantastic stretch drive, a one-game playoff win at Boston, a pennant victory over Kansas City and a World Series triumph over the Dodgers were overshadowed by a mid-season hassle involving Reggie Jackson, owner George Steinbrenner and manager Billy Martin.

The result was Martin's tearful resignation in late July and the hiring of Bob Lemon, who skippered the club to its eventual storybook victory. Trailing the Red Sox by 14 games on July 19, five days prior to Martin's demise, the Yankees launched one of the game's greatest surges, winning 52 of 73, to set up the divisional title win at Boston which was followed by the flag and Series triumphs.

Ron Guidry's amazing 25-3 season, which included a league-leading 1.74 ERA, won him the coveted Cy Young Award. Ed Figueroa was 20-9, Catfish Hunter 12-6 and Rich Gossage, out of the pen, won 10 plus 27 saves.

The controversial Jackson hit 27 home runs and had 97 RBIs, while Thurman Munson batted .297 and Graig Nettles had 27 four-baggers and 93 RBIs. Lou Piniella contributed a .314 average, built on one timely basehit after another.

P
Yankees
ED FIGUEROA

P
Yankees
RICH GOSSAGE

P
Yankees
RON GUIDRY

P
Yankees
DON GULLETT

C
Yankees
FRAN HEALY

P
Yankees
KEN HOLTZMAN

P
Yankees
JIM HUNTER

MOST HOMERS, ONE WORLD SERIES
'77 RECORD BREAKER
REGGIE JACKSON

A.L. ALL STAR OF
Yankees
REGGIE JACKSON

WORLD SERIES
REGGIE & YANKEES REIGN SUPREME

DH-C-1B
Yankees
CLIFF JOHNSON

MOST GAMES, PURE RELIEF, LIFETIME
'77 RECORD BREAKER
SPARKY LYLE

P
Yankees
SPARKY LYLE

AS MANAGER
AS PLAYER
BILLY MARTIN
Yankees

C
Yankees
THURMAN MUNSON

3B
Yankees
GRAIG NETTLES

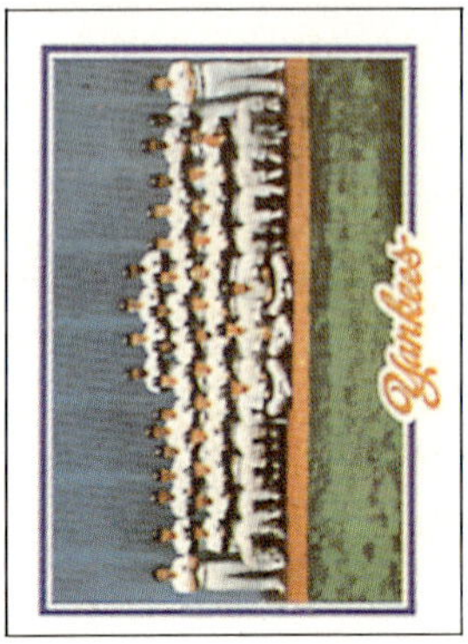

1979

What might have been another victorious year for the Yankees in 1979 became one of tragedy and disappointment when Thurman Munson perished in the crash of a plane he was flying near his Canton, Ohio, home in August.

However, long before Munson's grievous loss, the chances of the Yankees repeating as champions began fading after bullpen ace Rich Gossage suffered a thumb injury in a clubhouse scuffle with teammate Cliff Johnson in April.

Gossage missed 83 games and by the time he returned, to win five and save 18, the Yankees' dream of conquest was shattered as they sank to fourth place. Even the return of Billy Martin as Bob Lemon's replacement in June failed to rouse the reeling ballclub.

Reggie Jackson hit 29 home runs and drove in 89 runs, while Lou Piniella hit .297 and Graig Nettles had 20 homers and 73 RBIs. As to pitching, Ron Guidry (18-8) was again the league's ERA leader with a 2.78. Free agent lefty Tommy John was 21-9, but the ailing Catfish Hunter bowed out with a 2-9 record and the sore-armed Ed Figueroa was 4-6.

JIM BEATTIE P
YANKEES

PAUL BLAIR OF
YANKEES

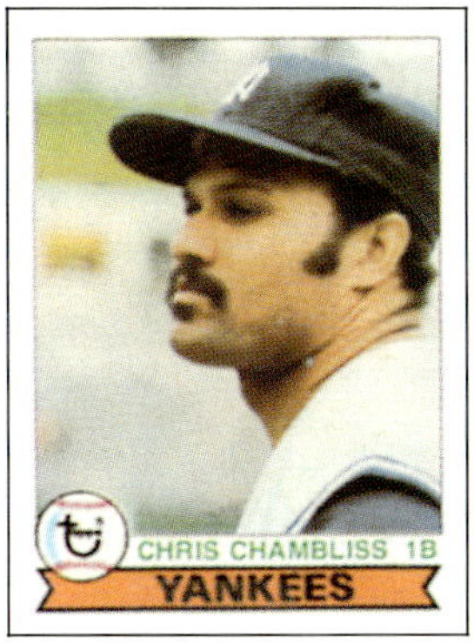
CHRIS CHAMBLISS 1B
YANKEES

KEN CLAY P
YANKEES

BUCKY DENT SS
YANKEES

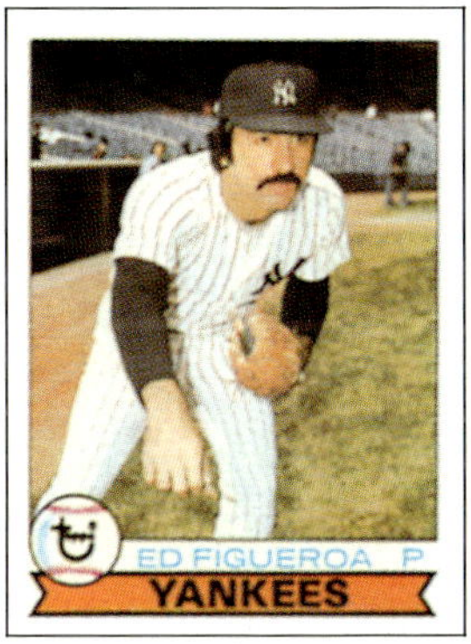
ED FIGUEROA P
YANKEES

RICH GOSSAGE P
YANKEES

1978 RECORD BREAKER
RON GUIDRY
American League Record: Most Strikeouts, Lefthander, 9-inning Game

RON GUIDRY P
YANKEES

DON GULLETT P
YANKEES

JIM HUNTER P
YANKEES

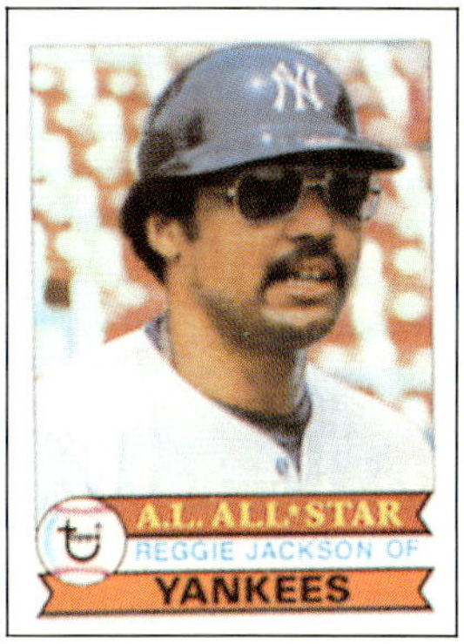
A.L. ALL-STAR
REGGIE JACKSON OF
YANKEES

CLIFF JOHNSON DH-C
YANKEES

JAY JOHNSTONE OF
YANKEES

PAUL LINDBLAD P
YANKEES

SPARKY LYLE P
YANKEES

ANDY MESSERSMITH P
YANKEES

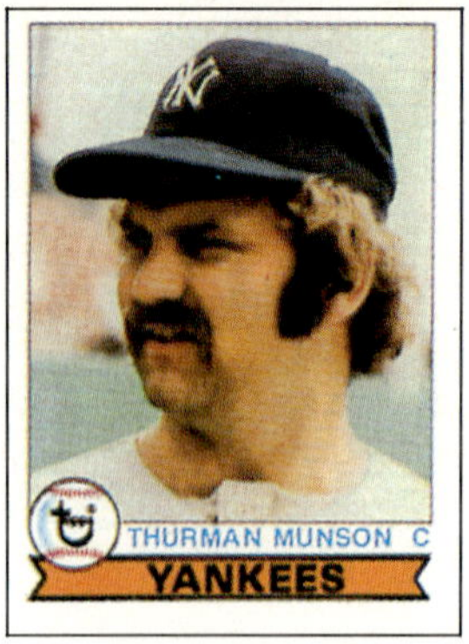
THURMAN MUNSON C
YANKEES

GRAIG NETTLES 3B
YANKEES

LOU PINIELLA OF
YANKEES

WILLIE RANDOLPH 2B
YANKEES

MICKEY RIVERS OF
YANKEES

JIM SPENCER DH-1B
YANKEES

FRED STANLEY SS-3B
YANKEES

GARY THOMASSON OF-1B
YANKEES

DICK TIDROW P
YANKEES

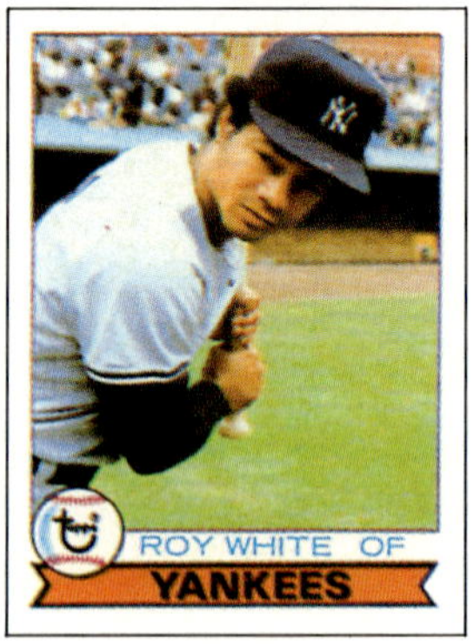
ROY WHITE OF
YANKEES

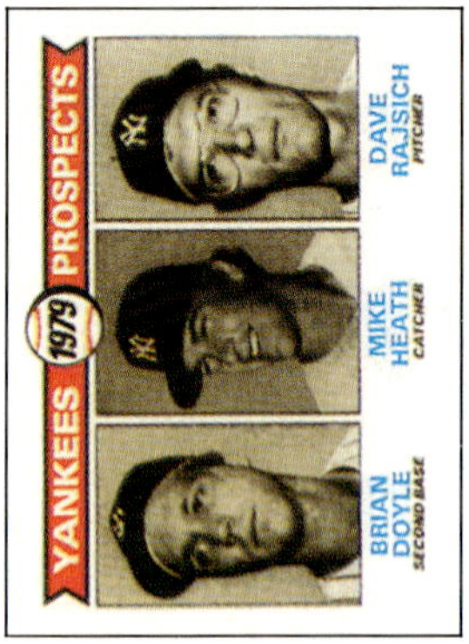
YANKEES 1979 PROSPECTS
DAVE RAJSICH PITCHER
MIKE HEATH CATCHER
BRIAN DOYLE SECOND BASE

YANKEES
BOB LEMON
MANAGER

1980

It was another of those seasons when the Yankees did everything but win the American League flag. They won 103 games to capture the Eastern Division title, but a three-straight sweep by Kansas City in the pennant playoff prompted the "resignation" of manager Dick Howser.

Free agent acquisition Bob Watson led the club with a .307 average and Reggie Jackson, a .300 hitter, tied for the league's home run title with 41. Rick Cerone, acquired from Toronto to replace Thurman Munson, hit .277 with 14 homers and 85 RBIs.

Southpaw Tommy John pitched to a 22-9 record, while Rudy May, another free agent acquisition, was 15-5 and his 2.46 ERA was the best in the league. Rich Gossage, again the supreme reliever, posted 33 saves and a 2.27 ERA while striking out 103 batters in 99 innings.

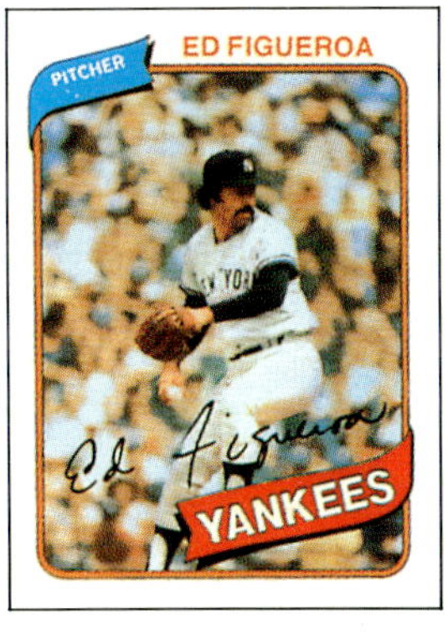

DES. HITTER
OSCAR GAMBLE
YANKEES

PITCHER
RICH GOSSAGE
YANKEES

PITCHER
RON GUIDRY
YANKEES
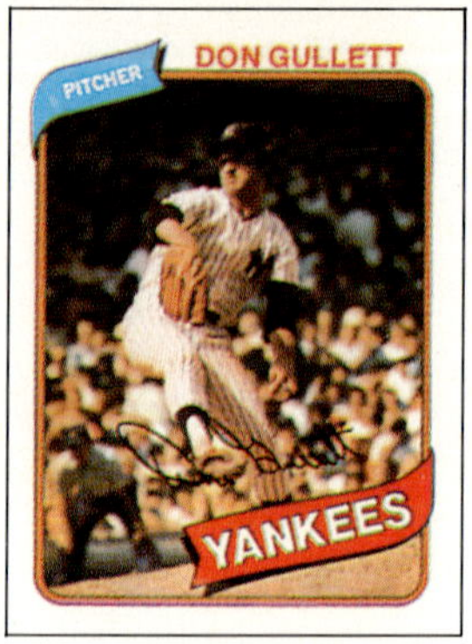
PITCHER
DON GULLETT
YANKEES

PITCHER
DON HOOD
YANKEES

OUTFIELD
REGGIE JACKSON
YANKEES

PITCHER
TOMMY JOHN
YANKEES

PITCHER
JIM KAAT
YANKEES

OUTFIELD
BOBBY MURCER
YANKEES
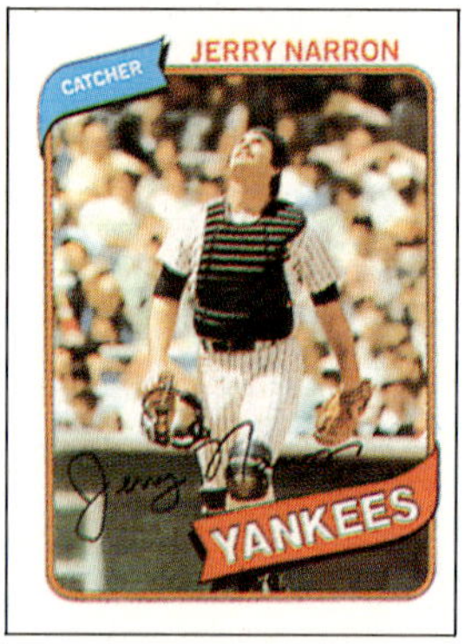
CATCHER
JERRY NARRON
YANKEES

3rd BASE
GRAIG NETTLES
YANKEES

OUTFIELD
LOU PINIELLA
YANKEES

2nd BASE
WILLIE RANDOLPH
YANKEES

1st BASE
GEORGE SCOTT
YANKEES

DH-1B
JIM SPENCER
YANKEES

SS-3B
FRED STANLEY
YANKEES

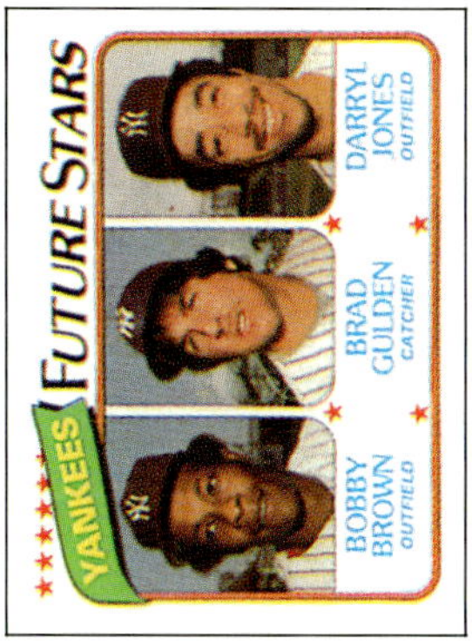

1981

The 1981 season, interrupted on June 12 by a 50-day strike of major league players, is one baseball will long remember and Yankees owner George Steinbrenner wants to forget. With Gene Michael serving as manager, the Yankees were in first place in their division when the work stoppage began.

When play finally resumed in August, Commissioner Bowie Kuhn ruled the season would be split and the clubs that led the first half would qualify for the mini-playoffs that followed the second segment.

The Yankees, 34-22 when the strike started, were 25-26 in the second and Steinbrenner, irked by their sluggish performance, replaced Michael with Bob Lemon in September. Dave Winfield, the $21 million free agent, batted .294 with 68 RBIs and Jerry Mumphrey hit .307. The Yankees defeated Milwaukee for the East title and wiped out the Billy Martin-led A's for the pennant.

Ron Guidry won 11 and Tommy John nine. Rookie of the Year Dave Righetti was 8-4. But it was all dismissed when the Dodgers, rebounding from an 0-2 deficit, won the Series in six games and Steinbrenner apologized to New York "and Yankees fans everywhere."

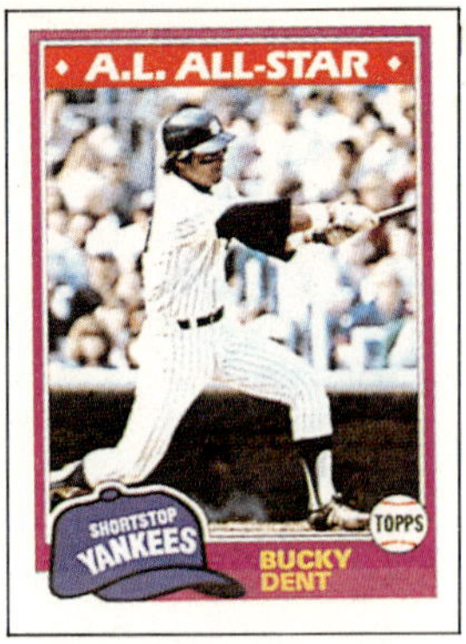
A.L. ALL-STAR
SHORTSTOP
YANKEES
TOPPS
BUCKY DENT

2nd BASE
YANKEES
TOPPS
BRIAN DOYLE

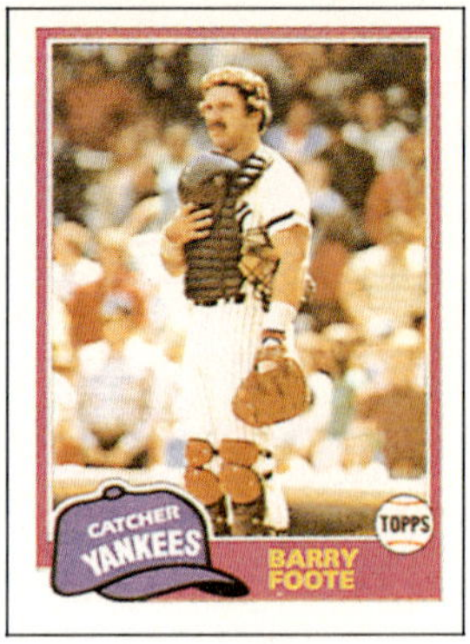
CATCHER
YANKEES
TOPPS
BARRY FOOTE

DH-OF
YANKEES
TOPPS
OSCAR GAMBLE

A.L. ALL-STAR
PITCHER
YANKEES
TOPPS
RICH GOSSAGE

PITCHER
YANKEES
TOPPS
MIKE GRIFFIN

PITCHER
YANKEES
TOPPS
RON GUIDRY

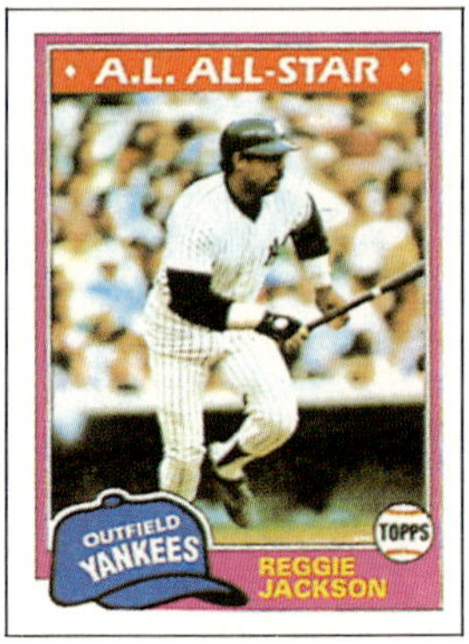
A.L. ALL-STAR
OUTFIELD
YANKEES
TOPPS
REGGIE JACKSON

PITCHER
YANKEES
TOPPS
TOMMY JOHN

OUTFIELD
YANKEES
TOPPS
RUPPERT JONES

PITCHER
YANKEES
TOPPS
DAVE LaROCHE

OUTFIELD
YANKEES
TOPPS
JOE LEFEBVRE

PITCHER
YANKEES
TOPPS
RUDY MAY

SS-2B
YANKEES
TOPPS
LARRY MILBOURNE

OUTFIELD
YANKEES
TOPPS
JERRY MUMPHREY

OUTFIELD
YANKEES
TOPPS
BOBBY MURCER

PITCHER
YANKEES
GENE NELSON
TOPPS

3rd BASE
YANKEES
GRAIG NETTLES
TOPPS

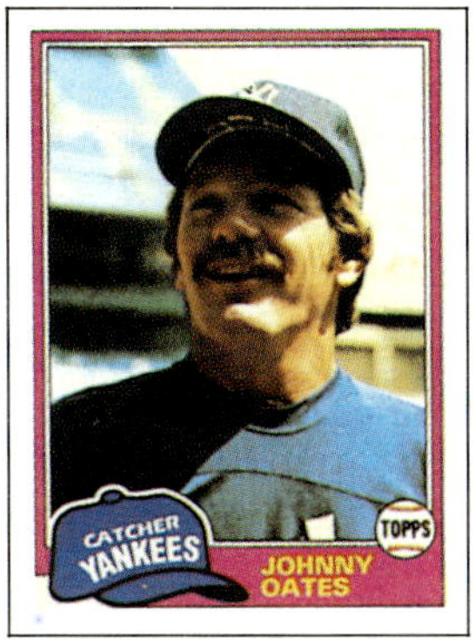
CATCHER
YANKEES
JOHNNY OATES
TOPPS

PITCHER
YANKEES
GAYLORD PERRY
TOPPS

OUTFIELD
YANKEES
LOU PINIELLA
TOPPS

2nd BASE
YANKEES
WILLIE RANDOLPH
TOPPS

PITCHER
YANKEES
RICK REUSCHEL
TOPPS

1st BASE
YANKEES
DAVE REVERING
TOPPS

3rd BASE
YANKEES
AURELIO RODRIGUEZ
TOPPS

DH-3B
YANKEES
ERIC SODERHOLM
TOPPS

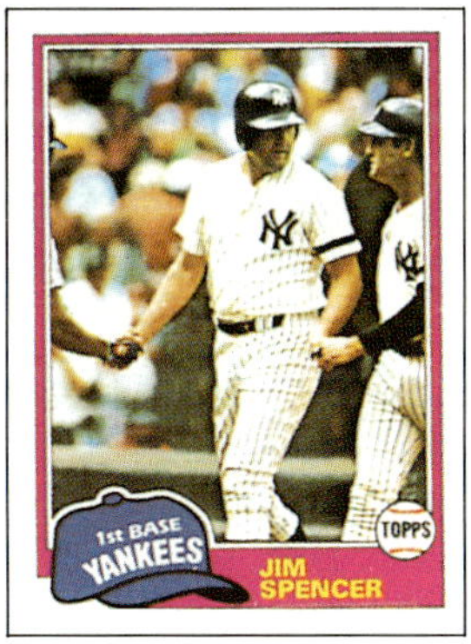
1st BASE
YANKEES
JIM SPENCER
TOPPS

SS-3B-2B
YANKEES
FRED STANLEY
TOPPS

PITCHER
YANKEES
LUIS TIANT
TOPPS

PITCHER
YANKEES
TOM UNDERWOOD
TOPPS

1st BASE
YANKEES
BOB WATSON
TOPPS

OUTFIELD
YANKEES
DAVE WINFIELD
TOPPS

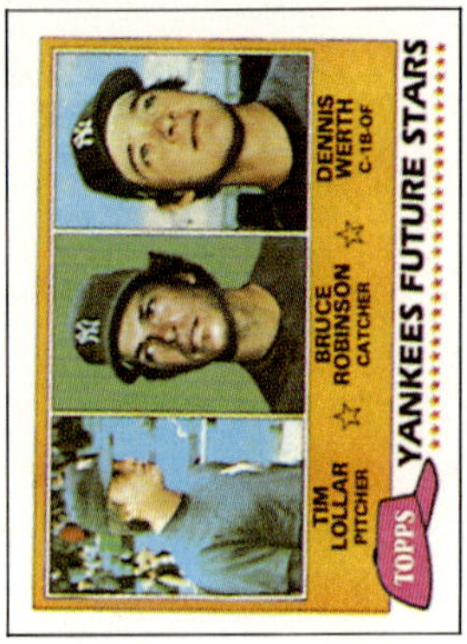

1982

What Yankees owner George Steinbrenner reckoned would be "the best balanced team in my 10 years here," turned out to be considerably less as the 1982 edition sank to fifth place. Manager Bob Lemon, fired on April 25, Gene Michael, fired on Aug. 3, and Clyde King, who finished the season, shared the pilothouse.

Reggie Jackson, Bob Watson, Bucky Dent and Tommy John became ex-Yankees, while Dave Winfield batted .280 with 37 homers and 106 RBIs. Jerry Mumphrey batted .300 and Lou Piniella .307. Ken Griffey, another expensive free agent , hit .277.

The pitching was in and out with Ron Guidry (14-8), Dave Righetti (11-10) and Shane Rawley (11-10) being the most consistent. Ace reliever Rich Gossage, who spent considerable time feuding with Steinbrenner, produced 30 saves despite missing more than a month because of tendinitis.

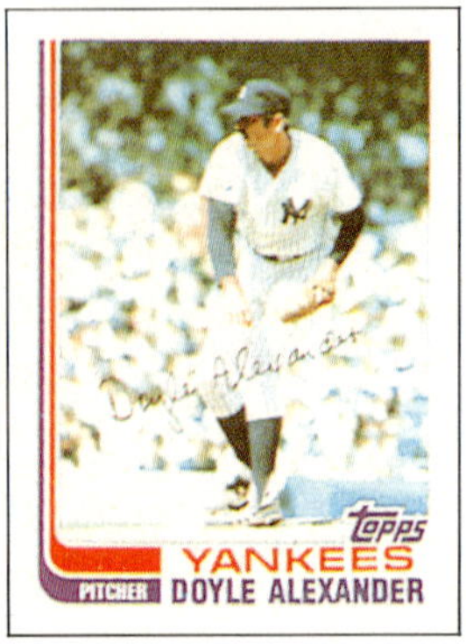

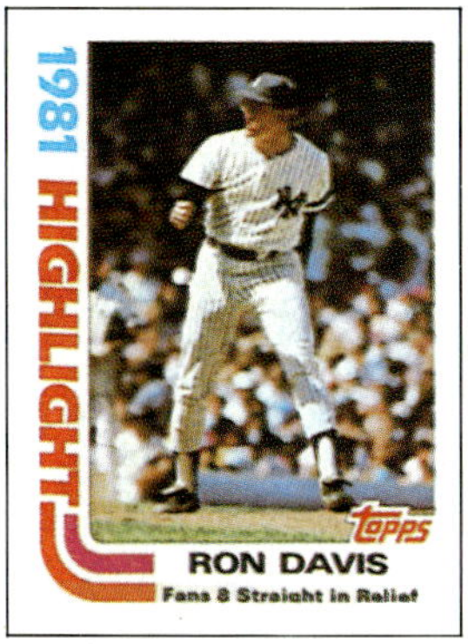
1981 HIGHLIGHT
topps
RON DAVIS
Fans 8 Straight in Relief

topps
YANKEES
PITCHER
RON DAVIS

topps
YANKEES
SHORTSTOP
BUCKY DENT

BUCKY DENT
topps
in action

topps
A.L.
ALL STAR
SHORTSTOP
BUCKY DENT

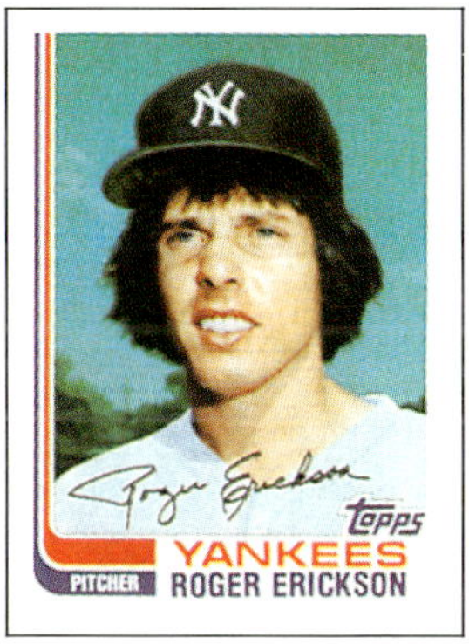
topps
YANKEES
PITCHER
ROGER ERICKSON

topps
YANKEES
CATCHER
BARRY FOOTE

topps
YANKEES
PITCHER
GEORGE FRAZIER

topps
YANKEES
DH-OF
OSCAR GAMBLE

topps
A.L.
ALL STAR
RELIEVER
RICH GOSSAGE

topps
YANKEES
PITCHER
RICH GOSSAGE

RICH GOSSAGE
topps
in action

topps
YANKEES
OUTFIELD
KEN GRIFFEY

topps
YANKEES
PITCHER
RON GUIDRY

RON GUIDRY
topps
in action

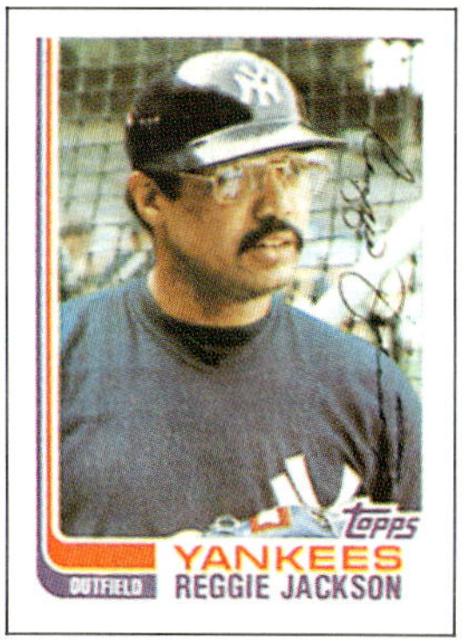
topps
YANKEES
OUTFIELD
REGGIE JACKSON

REGGIE JACKSON
topps
in action

topps
YANKEES
PITCHER
TOMMY JOHN

topps
YANKEES
PITCHER
DAVE LaROCHE

topps
YANKEES
PITCHER
RUDY MAY

topps
YANKEES
1st BASE
JOHN MAYBERRY

topps
YANKEES
3B-SS-2B
LARRY MILBOURNE

topps
YANKEES
OUTFIELD
JERRY MUMPHREY

topps
YANKEES
OUTFIELD
BOBBY MURCER

topps
YANKEES
PITCHER
GENE NELSON

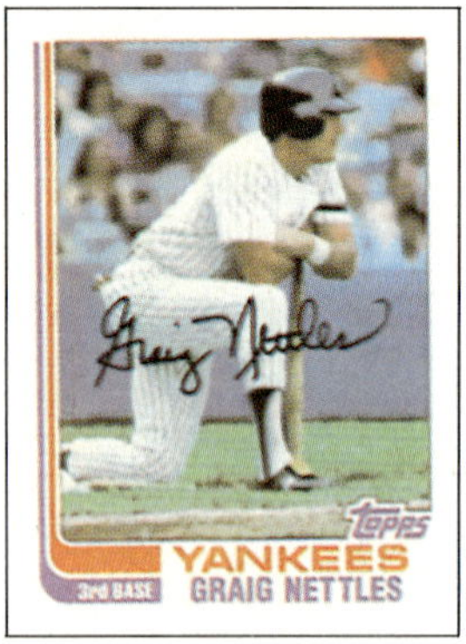
topps
YANKEES
3rd BASE
GRAIG NETTLES

GRAIG NETTLES
topps
in action

topps
YANKEES
OUTFIELD
LOU PINIELLA

topps
A.L.
ALL STAR
2nd BASE
WILLIE RANDOLPH

topps
YANKEES
2nd BASE
WILLIE RANDOLPH

WILLIE RANDOLPH
topps
in action

topps
YANKEES
PITCHER
SHANE RAWLEY

topps
YANKEES
PITCHER
RICK REUSCHEL

topps
YANKEES
1st BASE
DAVE REVERING

topps
YANKEES
PITCHER
DAVE RIGHETTI

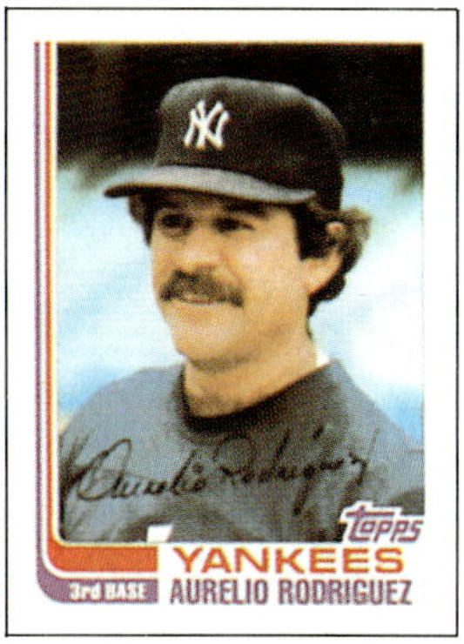
topps
YANKEES
3rd BASE
AURELIO RODRIGUEZ

topps
YANKEES
SS-3B
ROY SMALLEY

topps
YANKEES
1st BASE
BOB WATSON

topps
YANKEES
PITCHER
DAVE WEHRMEISTER

topps
YANKEES
C-1B-OF
DENNIS WERTH

topps
YANKEES
OUTFIELD
DAVE WINFIELD

topps
YANKEES
CATCHER
BUTCH WYNEGAR

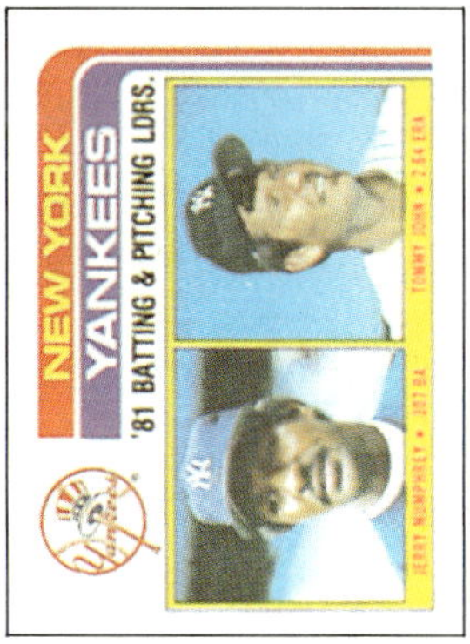
NEW YORK
YANKEES
'81 BATTING & PITCHING LDRS.
JERRY MUMPHREY • .307 BA
TOMMY JOHN • 2.64 ERA

STEVE BALBONI
1st Base
ANDY McGAFFIGAN
Pitcher
ANDRE ROBERTSON
Shortstop
NEW YORK YANKEES
FUTURE STARS
topps

1983

It was the controversial Billy Martin's turn to manage the Yankees in 1983 and his best efforts, most of which were marred by costly injuries, resulted in a third-place windup.

Dave Winfield batted .283 with 32 homers and 116 runs batted in and Graig Nettles hit 20 home runs and had 75 RBIs for his best output since 1978. Despite a hamstring that idled him for six weeks, Ken Griffey hit .306, but $5.45-million free agent Steve Kemp hit only .241 with a dozen homers.

Ron Guidry and fellow lefty Dave Righetti provided some quality pitching. Guidry was 21-9 and Righetti, who no-hit Boston on July 4, was 14-8. Shane Rawley finished at 14-14, but Rudy May, bothered by ailments, lost five of six decisions.

Rich Gossage again was the bullpen star, but his numbers weren't those of prior seasons. He won 13 and had 22 saves in what was his final season at the Stadium. Righty reliever George Frazier supported Gossage with eight rescues.

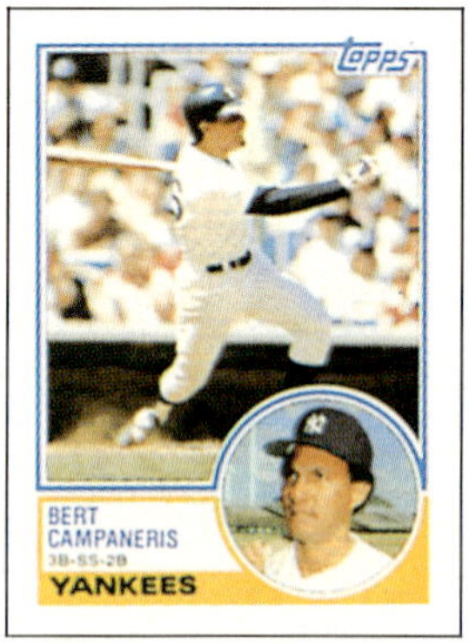

GEORGE
FRAZIER
PITCHER
YANKEES

OSCAR
GAMBLE
DH-OUTFIELD
YANKEES

RICH
GOSSAGE
PITCHER
YANKEES

SUPER VETERAN
1983
1972
RICH GOSSAGE

KEN
GRIFFEY
OUTFIELD
YANKEES

RON
GUIDRY
PITCHER
YANKEES

BUTCH
HOBSON
3rd BASE-1st BASE
YANKEES

STEVE
KEMP
OUTFIELD
YANKEES

MATT
KEOUGH
PITCHER
YANKEES

CLYDE KING
MANAGER
NEW YORK YANKEES

DAVE
LaROCHE
PITCHER
YANKEES

SUPER VETERAN
1983
1970
DAVE LaROCHE

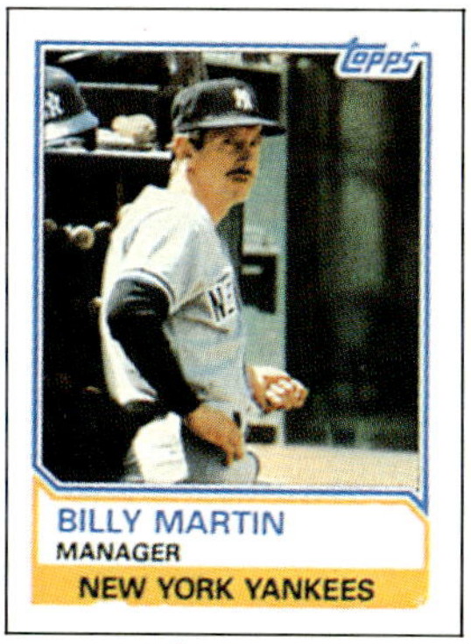
BILLY MARTIN
MANAGER
NEW YORK YANKEES

RUDY
MAY
PITCHER
YANKEES

JOHN
MAYBERRY
1st BASE
YANKEES

LEE
MAZZILLI
OUTFIELD-1st BASE
YANKEES

MIKE
MORGAN
PITCHER
YANKEES

JERRY
MUMPHREY
OUTFIELD
YANKEES

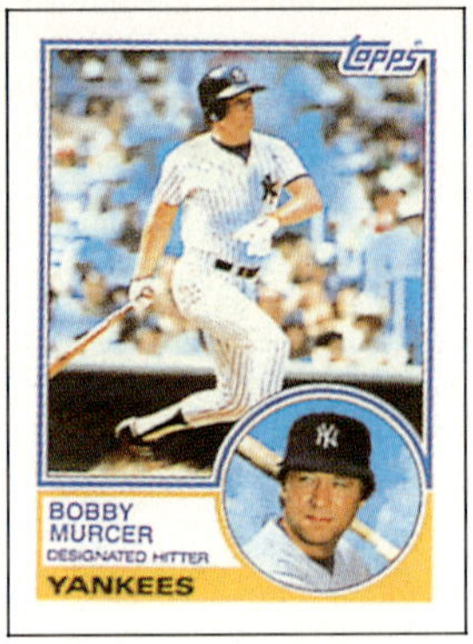
BOBBY
MURCER
DESIGNATED HITTER
YANKEES

SUPER VETERAN
1983
1965
BOBBY MURCER

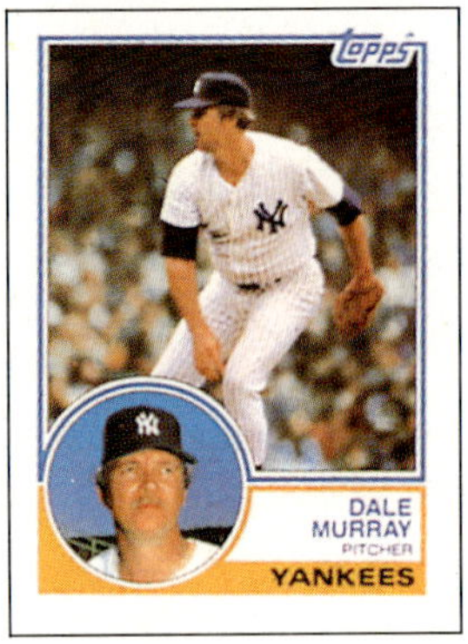
DALE
MURRAY
PITCHER
YANKEES

GRAIG
NETTLES
3rd BASE
YANKEES

SUPER VETERAN
1983
1967
GRAIG NETTLES

LOU
PINIELLA
OUTFIELD
YANKEES

WILLIE
RANDOLPH
2nd BASE
YANKEES

SHANE
RAWLEY
PITCHER
YANKEES

DAVE
RIGHETTI
PITCHER
YANKEES

ANDRE
ROBERTSON
SS-2nd BASE
YANKEES

BOB
SHIRLEY
PITCHER
YANKEES

ROY
SMALLEY
SS-3rd BASE
YANKEES

DAVE
WINFIELD
OUTFIELD
YANKEES

BUTCH
WYNEGAR
CATCHER
YANKEES

1984

The ever popular Yogi Berra was the Yankees' skipper in 1984 and though the club finished third, 17 games behind Detroit, Berra was optimistic because of his club's second-half surge.

Dave Winfield and Don Mattingly contended for the American League batting title, which the latter won on the final day with .343 to Winfield's .340. Mattingly also hit 23 homers and had 110 runs batted in. Designated hitter Don Baylor propelled 27 homers and knocked home 89 runs.

The pitching was dominated by ageless knuckleballer Phil Niekro, who won 16 and lost eight. Newcomer Joe Cowley finished at 9-2 and Jay Howell 9-4. Ron Guidry's best was 10-11. Dave Righetti, shifted to the 'pen to replace the departed Rich Gossage, won five and saved 31 others. Fans and the so-called "experts" argued loud and long about the lefty's shift from starter to reliever.

YANKEES
Topps
BERT CAMPANERIS
3B-SS-2B

YANKEES
Topps
RICK CERONE
C

YANKEES
Topps
TIM FOLI
SS

YANKEES
Topps
RAY FONTENOT
P

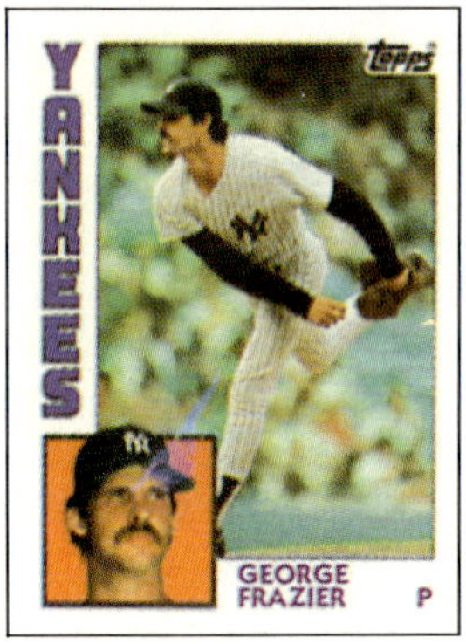
YANKEES
Topps
GEORGE FRAZIER
P

YANKEES
Topps
OSCAR GAMBLE
DH-OF

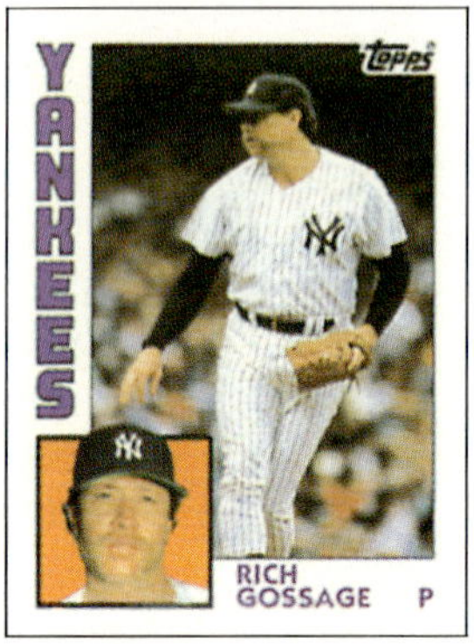
YANKEES
Topps
RICH GOSSAGE
P

YANKEES
Topps
KEN GRIFFEY
OF-1B

YANKEES
Topps
RON GUIDRY
P

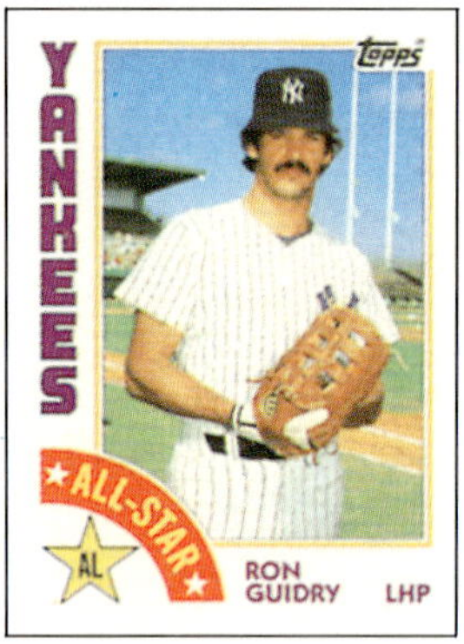
YANKEES
Topps
ALL-STAR
AL
RON GUIDRY
LHP

YANKEES
Topps
TOBY HARRAH
3B

YANKEES
Topps
JAY HOWELL
P

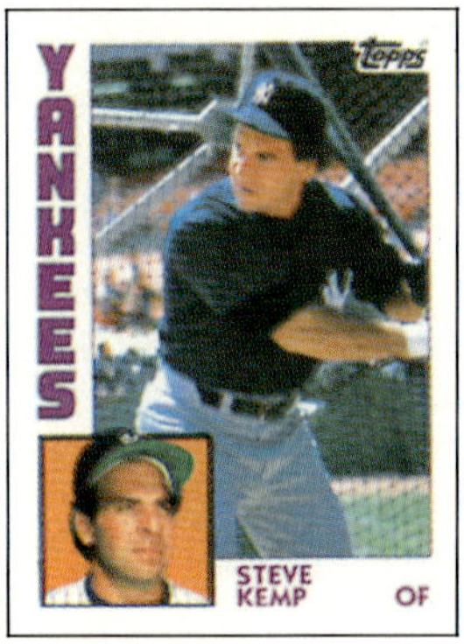
YANKEES
Topps
STEVE KEMP
OF

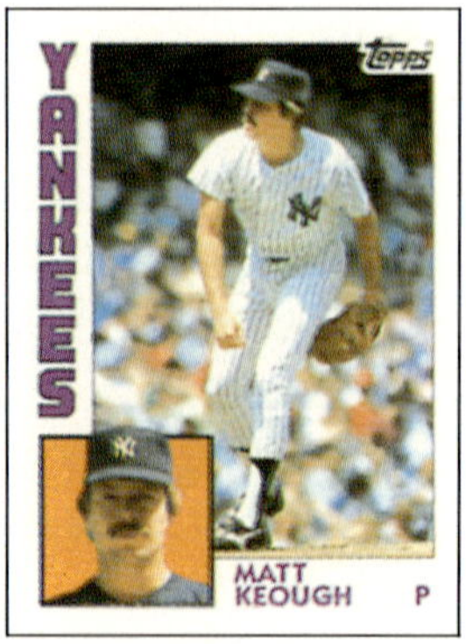
YANKEES
Topps
MATT KEOUGH
P

YANKEES
Topps
MANAGER
BILLY MARTIN

YANKEES
Topps
DON MATTINGLY
OF-1B

YANKEES
topps
RUDY MAY
P

YANKEES
topps
BOBBY MEACHAM
3B-SS

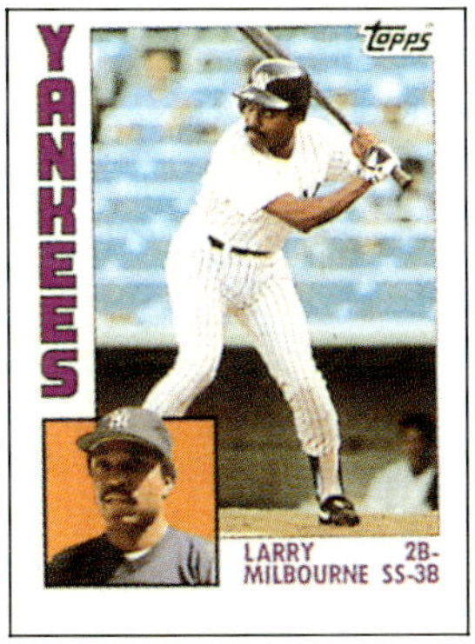
YANKEES
topps
LARRY MILBOURNE
2B-SS-3B

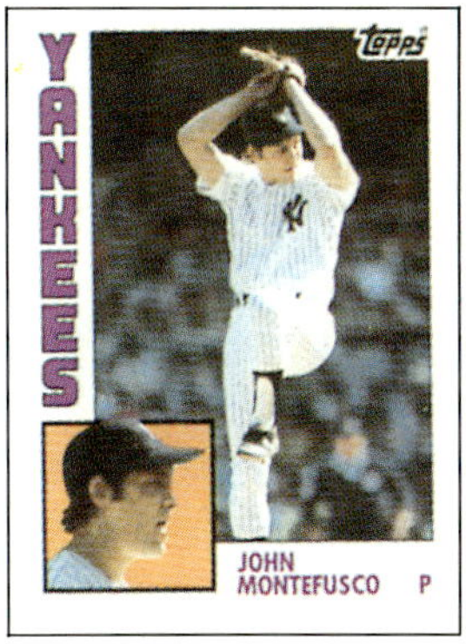
YANKEES
topps
JOHN MONTEFUSCO
P

YANKEES
topps
OMAR MORENO
OF

YANKEES
topps
DALE MURRAY
P

YANKEES
topps
GRAIG NETTLES
3B

YANKEES
topps
PHIL NIEKRO
P

YANKEES
topps
MIKE O'BERRY
C

YANKEES
topps
LOU PINIELLA
OF

YANKEES
topps
WILLIE RANDOLPH
2B

YANKEES
topps
SHANE RAWLEY
P

YANKEES
topps
DAVE RIGHETTI
P

YANKEES
topps
JOSE RIJO
P

YANKEES
topps
ANDRE ROBERTSON
SS-2B

YANKEES
topps
BOB SHIRLEY
P

1985

The Yankees again played musical managerial chairs in 1985 with Yogi Berra and Billy Martin, the latter making his fourth appearance in the dugout, to handle the ballclub. The Bombers finished second, two games behind Toronto, but many thought it a disappointing result.

Following a slow start that unseated Berra after just 16 games, the team worked its way back into contention and was a game and a half behind the Blue Jays on Sept. 12. But an eight-game slide occurred, and despite winning 10 of 12 at the end, the Yankees were eliminated on the next to last day of the schedule.

Don Mattingly was the MVP with his .324 average, 35 homers and league-leading 145 RBIs. Rickey Henderson batted .314 and stole 80 bases. Don Baylor hit 23 homers, while Dave Winfield batted .275 with 26 homers and 114 RBIs. Owner George Steinbrenner, however, was irked with the tall outfielder's late-season output.

Ron Guidry paced the pitchers with a 22-6 mark and Phil Niekro won 16, including his 300th career victory on the season's final day. Dave Righetti, at 12-7, had 28 saves and led the bullpen brigade.

YANKEES
P
MIKE ARMSTRONG

YANKEES
DH-OF
DON BAYLOR

YANKEES
MANAGER
YOGI BERRA

YANKEES
P
MARTY BYSTROM

YANKEES
C
RICK CERONE

YANKEES
P
CLAY CHRISTIANSEN

YANKEES
P
JOE COWLEY

YANKEES
OF
BRIAN DAYETT

YANKEES
SS
TIM FOLI

YANKEES
P
RAY FONTENOT

YANKEES
DH-OF
OSCAR GAMBLE

YANKEES
OF-1B
KEN GRIFFEY

YANKEES
P
RON GUIDRY

YANKEES
3B
TOBY HARRAH

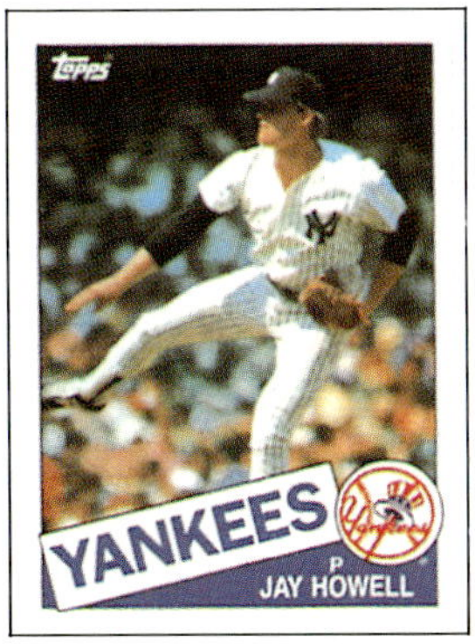
YANKEES
P
JAY HOWELL

YANKEES
OF
STEVE KEMP

YANKEES
1B
DON MATTINGLY

topps
YANKEES
SS
BOBBY MEACHAM

topps
YANKEES
P
JOHN MONTEFUSCO

topps
YANKEES
OF
OMAR MORENO

topps
YANKEES
P
DALE MURRAY

topps
YANKEES
P
PHIL NIEKRO

topps
YANKEES
3B
MIKE PAGLIARULO

topps
YANKEES
2B
WILLIE RANDOLPH

topps
YANKEES
P
DENNIS RASMUSSEN

topps
YANKEES
P
DAVE RIGHETTI

topps
YANKEES
P
JOSE RIJO

topps
YANKEES
SS
ANDRE ROBERTSON

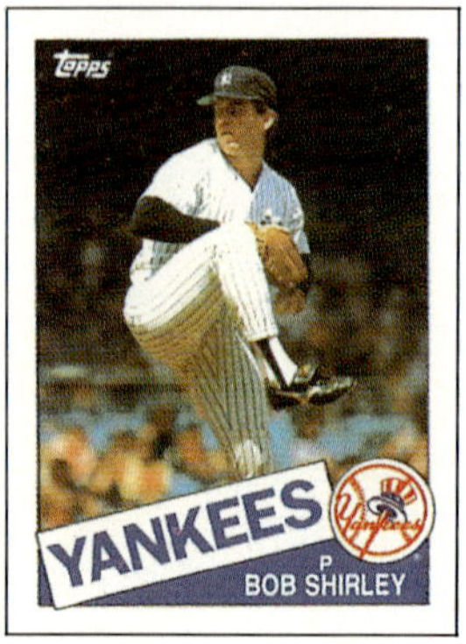
topps
YANKEES
P
BOB SHIRLEY

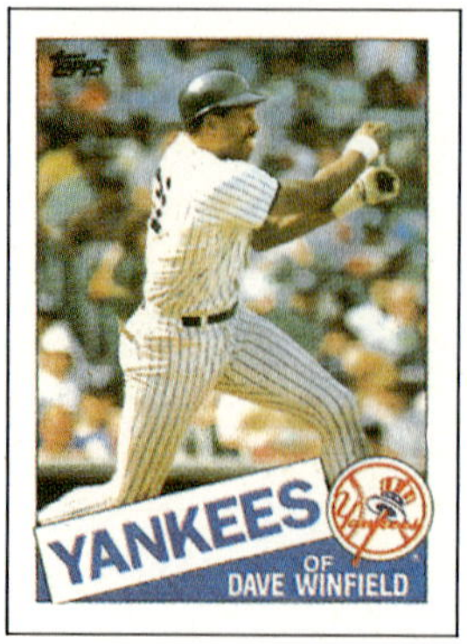
YANKEES
OF
DAVE WINFIELD

topps
DAVE WINFIELD
OUTFIELD
AL
ALL STAR

YANKEES
C
BUTCH WYNEGAR

1986

Despite finishing a surprising second to the Red Sox in the Eastern Division race, the Yankees' 1986 season wasn't exactly a day at the beach for rookie manager Lou Piniella. He had pitching problems from the outset. Also the failure to produce an everyday shortstop or an adequate replacement for Butch Wynegar after the veteran catcher left the club with emotional problems, prevented the Yankees from really contesting Boston.

Veterans Ron Guidry (9-12) and Joe Niekro (9-10) were pitching disappointments while Dave Righetti, with a record 46 saves, plus lefty Dennis Rasmussen (18-6) were pleasant surprises. Don Mattingly, batting .352 with 31 homers and 113 RBIs had yet another banner season. Mike Pagliarulo, despite a .238 average, slugged 28 homers and rookie Dan Pasqua, coming on in the second half, hit .293 with 16 homers. Dave Winfield, despite pressure from the front office, batted .262 with 24 home runs and 104 RBIs.

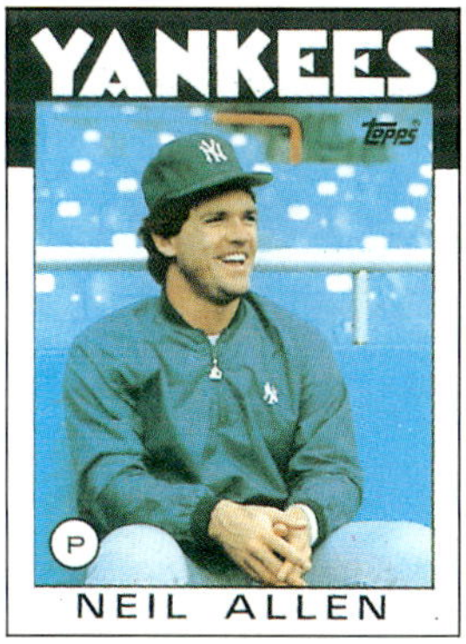

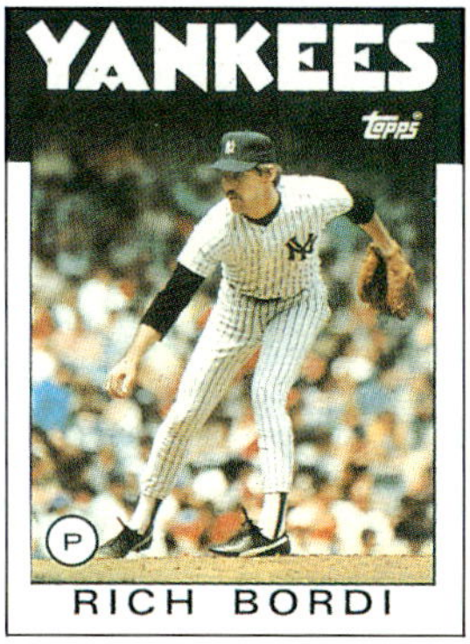

YANKEES
P
JOE COWLEY

YANKEES
P
BRIAN FISHER

YANKEES
OF-1B
KEN GRIFFEY

YANKEES
P
RON GUIDRY

RON GUIDRY
A.L. ALL STAR
P

YANKEES
C
RON HASSEY

YANKEES
C
RON HASSEY

YANKEES
OF
RICKEY HENDERSON

YANKEES
OF
RICKEY HENDERSON

RICKEY HENDERSON
A.L. ALL STAR
OF

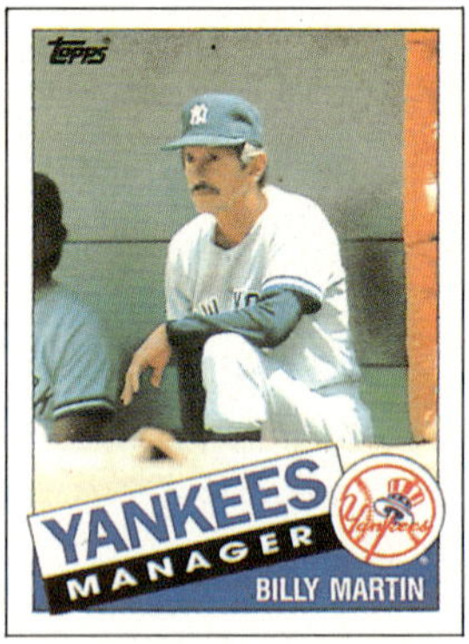
YANKEES
MANAGER
BILLY MARTIN

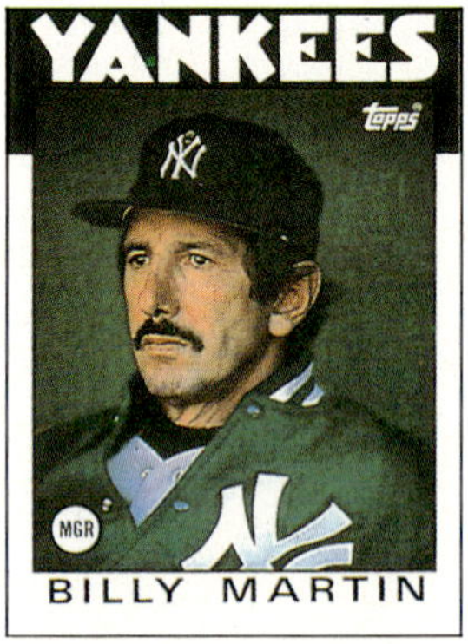
YANKEES
MGR
BILLY MARTIN

YANKEES
1B
DON MATTINGLY

DON MATTINGLY
A.L. ALL STAR
1B

YANKEES
SS
BOBBY MEACHAM

YANKEES
P
JOE NIEKRO

'85 RECORD BREAKER
PHIL NIEKRO, NEW YORK YANKEES
Oldest Pitcher to Hurl Shutout

YANKEES
P
PHIL NIEKRO

YANKEES
3B
MIKE PAGLIARULO

YANKEES
DH-OF
DAN PASQUA

YANKEES
2B
WILLIE RANDOLPH

YANKEES
P
DENNIS RASMUSSEN

YANKEES
P
DAVE RIGHETTI

YANKEES
SS-3B
ANDRE ROBERTSON

YANKEES
OF
BILLY SAMPLE

YANKEES
P
ROD SCURRY

YANKEES
P
BOB SHIRLEY

YANKEES
P
EDDIE WHITSON

YANKEES
P
EDDIE WHITSON

YANKEES
OF
DAVE WINFIELD

DAVE WINFIELD
A.L. ALL STAR
OF

YANKEES
C
BUTCH WYNEGAR

1987

Despite an 89-73 record, the Yankees' fourth place finish resulted in yet another managerial shift that moved Lou Piniella into the front office and returned Billy Martin to the dugout for the 1988 season.

Neither Don Mattingly nor Willie Randolph were responsible for the post-season moves. The All-Star first baseman hit a club-leading .327, with 30 home runs and 115 runs batted in. Randolph, still a stellar glove at second, chipped in with a career high .305 batting average.

Pitching contributed to the Yankees' downfall, with Rick Rhoden (16-13) the club's top winner. Tommy John, the 44-year-old lefthander was next with a 13-6 log. Except for Dave Righetti, who chalked 31 saves, the bullpen was an enduring puzzle.

Injuries, as usual, intruded on the club's plans for conquest. Speedster Rickey Henderson was limited to 95 games and only 41 stolen bases because of assorted ailments. Dave Winfield had 27 homers, the most he'd hit since 1983, but his 97 RBIs marked the first time since 1981 that his production failed to reach the century mark.

On July 4, at the midway mark of the season, the Yankees were 21 games over .500, but it was during the second half of the schedule they experienced the rocky going. They wound up 38-43 over the final 81 games, with a five-game losing streak in August adding greatly to their second-half woes.

JUAN
ESPINO

MIKE
FISCHLIN

BRIAN
FISHER

CECILIO
GUANTE

RON
GUIDRY

RICKEY
HENDERSON
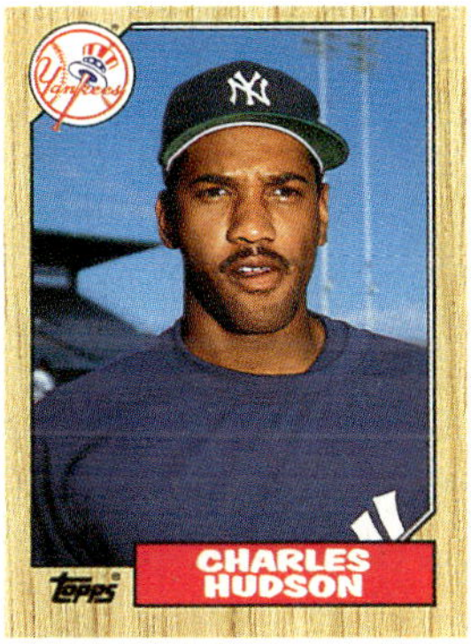
CHARLES
HUDSON

TOMMY
JOHN
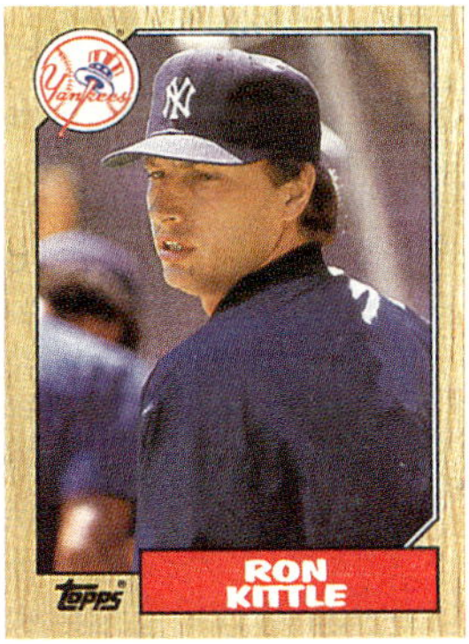
RON
KITTLE

DON
MATTINGLY

DON
MATTINGLY
ALL STAR

BOBBY
MEACHAM

JOE
NIEKRO
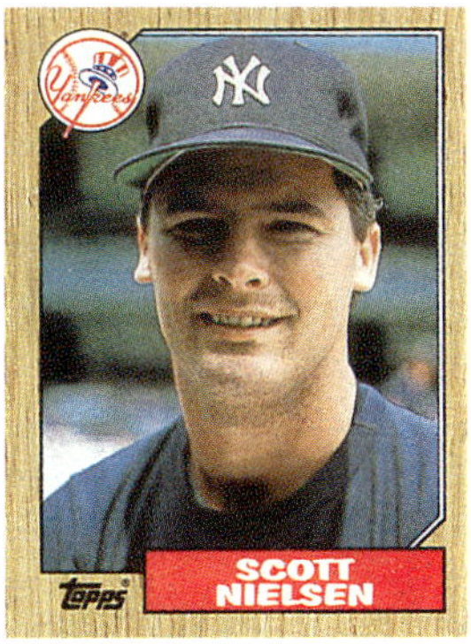
SCOTT
NIELSEN

MIKE
PAGLIARULO

DAN
PASQUA

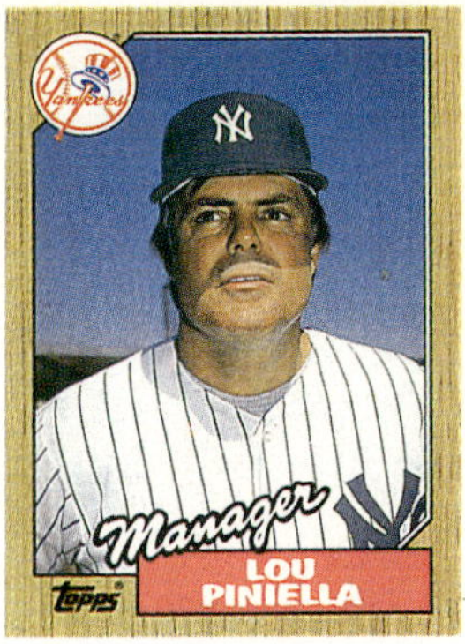
Manager
LOU
PINIELLA
topps

AL
PULIDO
topps

WILLIE
RANDOLPH
topps

DENNIS
RASMUSSEN
topps

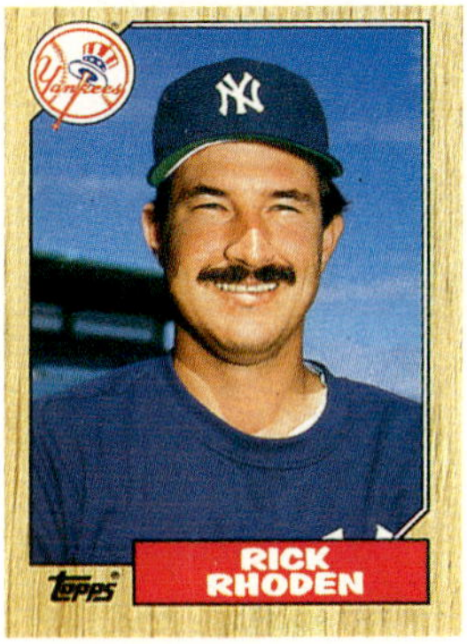
RICK
RHODEN
topps

DAVE
RIGHETTI
topps

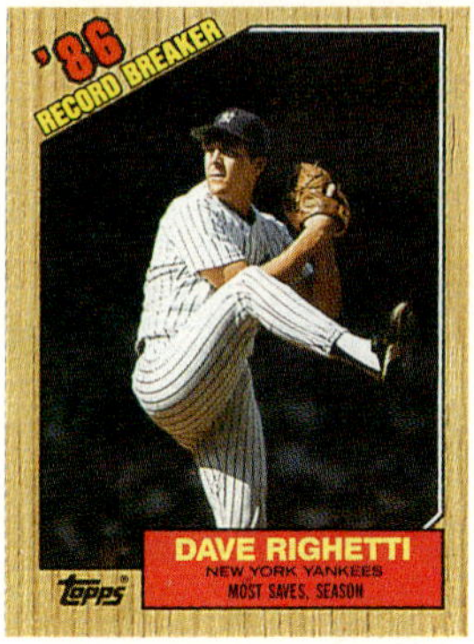
'86
RECORD BREAKER
DAVE RIGHETTI
NEW YORK YANKEES
MOST SAVES, SEASON
topps

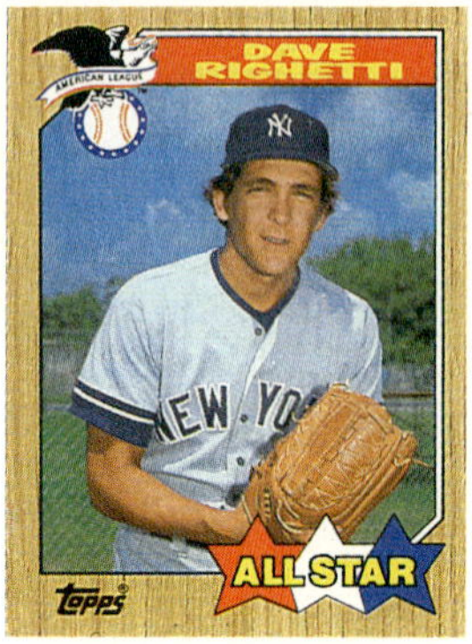
AMERICAN LEAGUE
DAVE
RIGHETTI
ALL STAR
topps

GARY
ROENICKE
topps

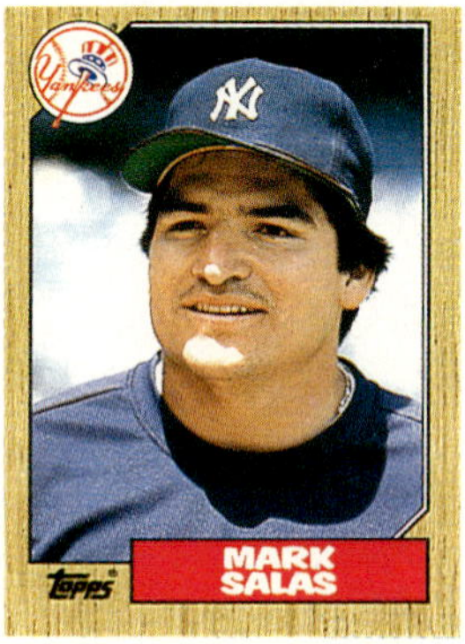
MARK
SALAS
topps

ROD
SCURRY
topps

BOB
SHIRLEY
topps

JOEL
SKINNER
topps

TIM
STODDARD
topps

BOB
TEWKSBURY
topps

WAYNE
TOLLESON
topps

GARY
WARD

CLAUDELL
WASHINGTON

DAVE
WINFIELD

BUTCH
WYNEGAR

PAUL
ZUVELLA

YANKEES LEADERS

1988

YANKEES
NEIL ALLEN
topps

YANKEES
BRAD ARNSBERG
topps

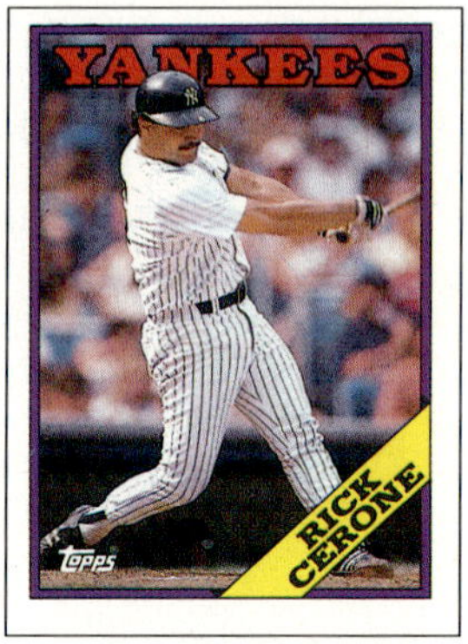
YANKEES
RICK CERONE
topps

YANKEES
PAT CLEMENTS
topps

YANKEES
HENRY COTTO
topps

YANKEES
MIKE EASLER
topps

YANKEES
CECILIO GUANTE
topps

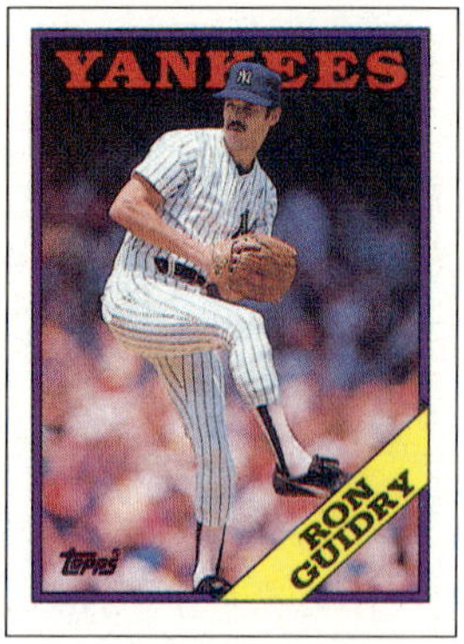
YANKEES
RON GUIDRY
topps

YANKEES
BILL GULLICKSON
topps

YANKEES
RICKEY HENDERSON
topps

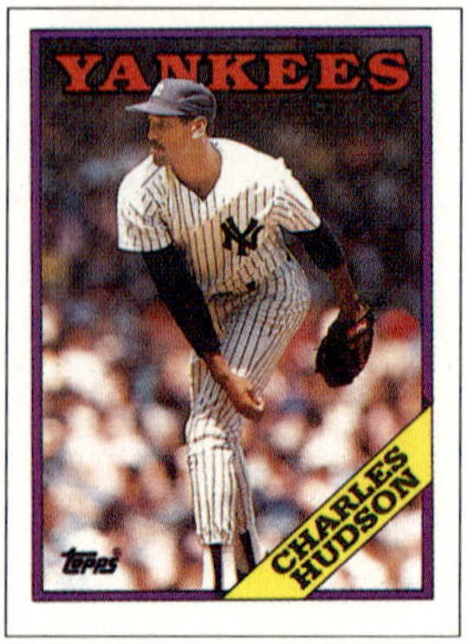
YANKEES
CHARLES HUDSON
topps

YANKEES
TOMMY JOHN
topps

RON KITTLE

Future Stars
AL LEITER

PHIL LOMBARDI

DON MATTINGLY

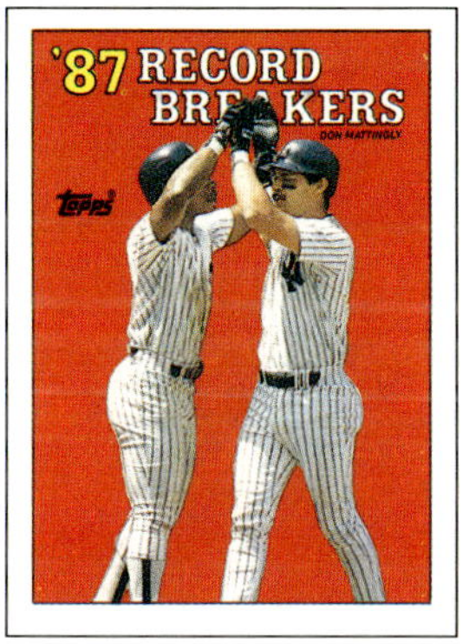
'87 RECORD
DON MATTINGLY

ALL STAR
American League
FIRST BASE
DON MATTINGLY

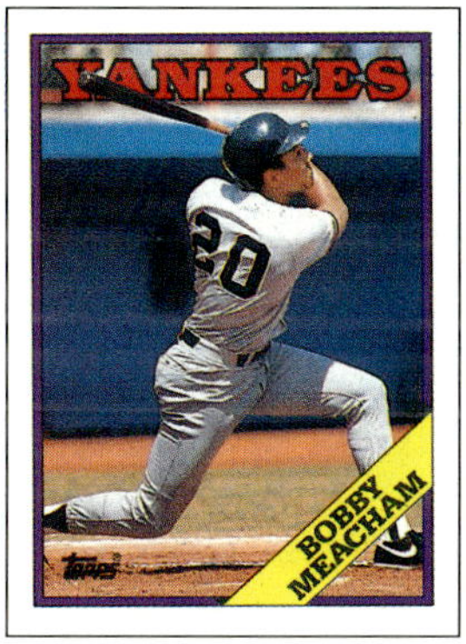
BOBBY MEACHAM

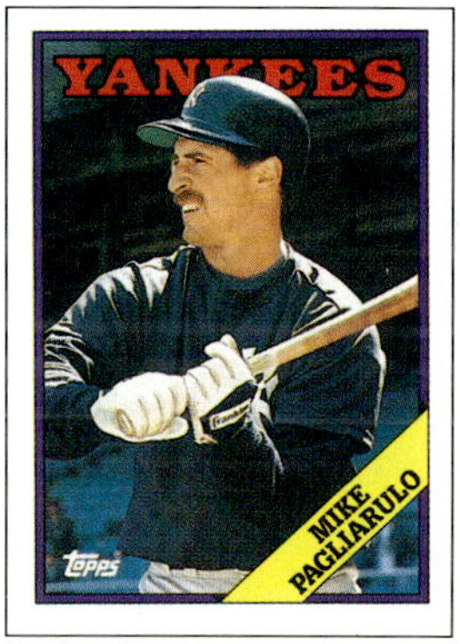
YANKEES
MIKE PAGLIARULO

DAN PASQUA

LOU PINIELLA
Manager

WILLIE RANDOLPH

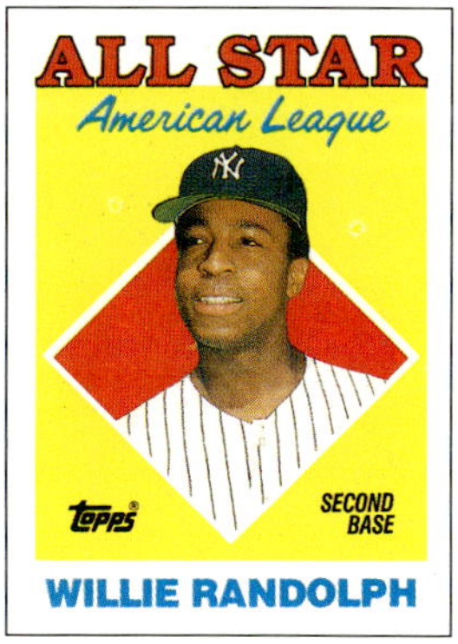
ALL STAR
American League
SECOND BASE
WILLIE RANDOLPH

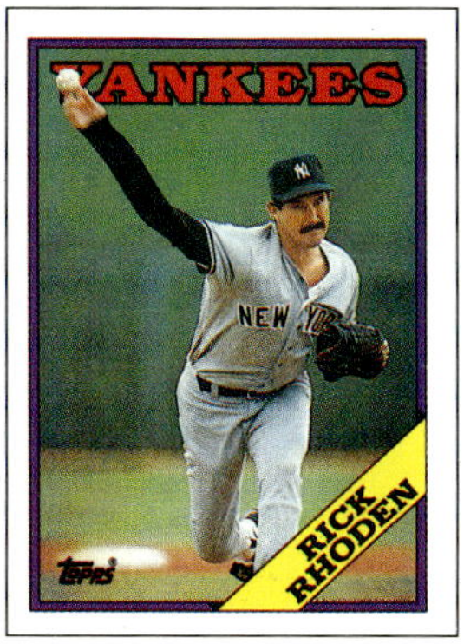
RICK RHODEN

DAVE RIGHETTI

JERRY ROYSTER

LENN SAKATA

YANKEES
JOEL SKINNER
topps

YANKEES
TIM STODDARD
topps

YANKEES
WAYNE TOLLESON
topps

YANKEES
STEVE TROUT
topps

YANKEES
GARY WARD
topps

YANKEES
CLAUDELL WASHINGTON

YANKEES
DAVE WINFIELD
topps

ALL STAR
American League
topps
OUTFIELD
DAVE WINFIELD

YANKEES
Leaders
topps

COLLECTORS' CORNER

1951: Blue Back of Johnny Mize (50) lists for $25 . . . Red Back of Duke Snider (38) lists for $18 . . . Complete set of 9 Team Cards lists for $900 . . . Complete set of 11 Connie Mack All-Stars lists for $2750 with Babe Ruth and Lou Gehrig listing for $700 each . . . Current All-Stars of Jim Konstanty, Robin Roberts and Eddie Stanky list for $4000 each . . . Complete set lists for $14,250.

1952: Mickey Mantle (311) is unquestionably the most sought-after post-war gum card, reportedly valued at $6,500-plus . . . Ben Chapman (391) is photo of Sam Chapman . . . Complete set lists in excess of $36,000.

1953: Mickey Mantle (82) and Willie Mays (244) list for $1,500 each . . . Set features first TOPPS card of Hall-of-Famer Whitey Ford (207) and only TOPPS card of Hall-of-Famer Satchel Paige (220). Pete Runnels (219) is photo of Don Johnson . . . Complete set lists for $9,500.

1954: Ted Williams is depicted on two cards (1 and 250) . . . Set features rookie cards of Hank Aaron (128), Ernie Banks (94) and Al Kaline (201) . . . Card of Aaron lists for $650 . . . Card of Willie Mays (90) lists for $200 . . . Complete set lists for $5,500.

1955: Set features rookie cards of Sandy Koufax (123), Harmon Killebrew (124) and Roberto Clemente (164) . . . The Clemente and Willie Mays (194) cards list for $425 each . . .Complete set lists for $3,900.

1956: Set features rookie cards of Hall-of-Famers Will Harridge (1), Warren Giles (2), Walter Alston (8) and Luis Aparicio (292) . . . Card of Mickey Mantle (135) lists for $650 . . . Card of Willie Mays (130) lists for $125 . . . Complete set lists for $4,000 . . . The Team Cards are found both dated (1955) and undated and are valued at $15 (dated) and more . . . There are two unnumbered Checklist Cards valued high.

1957: Set features rookie cards of Don Drysdale (18), Frank Robinson (35) and Brooks Robinson (328) . . . A reversal of photo negative made Hank Aaron (20) appear as a left-handed batter . . . Card of Mickey Mantle (95) lists for $600 . . . Cards of Brooks Robinson and Sandy Koufax (302) list for $275 each . . . Complete set lists for $4,800.

1958: Set features first TOPPS cards of Casey Stengel (475) and Stan Musial (476) . . . Mike McCormick (37) is photo of Ray Monzant . . . Milt Bolling (188) is photo of Lou Berberet . . . Bob Smith (226) is photo of Bobby Gene Smith . . . Card of Mickey Mantle (150) lists for $400 . . . Card of Ted Williams (1) lists for $325 . . . Complete set lists for $4,800.

1959: In a notable error, Lou Burdette (440) is shown posing as a left-handed pitcher . . . Set features rookie card of Bob Gibson (514) . . . Ralph Lumenti (316) is photo of Camilo Pascual . . . Card of Gibson lists for $200 . . . Card of Mickey Mantle (10) lists for $300 . . . Complete set lists for $3,000.

1960: A run of 32 consecutively numbered rookie cards (117-148) includes the first card of Carl Yastrzemski (148) . . . J.C. Martin (346) is photo of Gary Peters . . . Gary Peters (407) is photo of J.C. Martin . . . Card of Yastrzemski lists for $150 . . . Card of Mickey Mantle (350) lists for $300 . . . Complete set lists for $2,600.

1961: The Warren Spahn All-Star (589) should have been numbered 587 . . . Set features rookie cards of Billy Williams (141) and Juan Marichal (417) . . . Dutch Dotterer (332) is photo of his brother, Tommy . . . Card of Mickey Mantle (300) lists for $200 . . . Card of Carl Yastrzemski (287) lists for $90 . . . Complete set lists for $3,600.

1962: Set includes special Babe Ruth feature (135-144) . . . some Hal Reniff cards numbered 139 should be 159 . . . Set features rookie card of Lou Brock (387) . . . Gene Freese (205) is shown posing as a left-handed batter . . . Card of Mickey Mantle (200) lists for $325 . . . Card of Carl Yastrzemski (425) lists for $125 . . . Complete set lists for $3,300.

1963: Set features rookie card of Pete Rose (537), which lists for $500-plus . . . Bob Uecker (126) is shown posing as a left-handed batter . . . Don Landrum (113) is photo of Ron Santo . . . Eli Grba (231) is photo of Ryne Duren . . . Card of Mickey Mantlo (200) lists for $200 . . . Card of Lou Brock (472) lists for $75 . . . Complete set lists for $2,900.

1964: Set features rookie cards of Richie Allen (243), Tony Conigliaro (287) and Phil Niekro (541) . . . Lou Burdette is again shown posing as a left-handed pitcher . . . Bud Bloomfield (532) is photo of Jay Ward . . . Card of Pete Rose (125) lists for $150 . . . Card of Mickey Mantle (50) lists for $175 . . . Complete set lists for $1,600.

1965: Set features rookie cards of Dave Johnson (473), Steve Carlton (477) and Jim Hunter (526) . . . Lew Krausse (462) is photo of Pete Lovrich . . . Gene Freese (492) is again shown posing as a left-handed batter . . . Cards of Carlton and Pete Rose (207) list for $135 . . . Card of Mickey Mantle (350) lists for $300 . . . Complete set lists for $800.

1966: Set features rookie card of Jim Palmer (126) . . . For the third time (see 1962 and 1965) Gene Freese (319) is shown posing as a left-handed batter . . . Dick Ellsworth (447) is photo of Ken Hubbs (died February 13, 1964) . . . Card of Gaylord Perry (598) lists for $175 . . . Card of Willie McCovey (550) lists for $80 . . . Complete set lists for $2,500.

1967: Set features rookie cards of Rod Carew (569) and Tom Seaver (581) . . . Jim Fregosi (385) is shown posing as a left-handed batter . . . George Korince (72) is photo of James Brown but was later corrected on a second Korince card (526) . . . Card of Carew lists for $150 . . . Card of Maury Wills (570) lists for $65 . . . Complete set lists for $2,500.

1968: Set features rookie cards of Nolan Ryan (177) and Johnny Bench (247) . . . The special feature of The Sporting News All-Stars (361-380) includes eight players in the Hall of Fame . . . Card of Ryan lists for $135 . . . Card of Bench lists for $125 . . . Complete set lists for $1,200.

1969: Set features rookie card of Reggie Jackson (260) . . . There are two poses each for Clay Dalrymple (151) and Donn Clendenon (208) . . . Aurelio Rodriguez (653) is photo of Lenny Garcia (Angels' bat boy) . . . Card of Mickey Mantle (500) lists for $150 . . . Card of Jackson lists for $175 . . . Complete set lists for $1,200.

1970: Set features rookie cards of Vida Blue (21), Thurman Munson (189) and Bill Buckner (286) . . . Also included are two deceased players Miguel Fuentes (88) and Paul Edmondson (414) who died after cards went to press . . . Card of Johnny Bench (660) lists for $75 . . . Card of Pete Rose (580) lists for $75 . . . Complete set lists for $1,000.

1971: Set features rookie card of Steve Garvey (341) . . . the final series (644-752) is found in lesser quantity and includes rookie card (664) of three pitchers named Reynolds (Archie, Bob and Ken) . . . Card of Garvey lists for $65 . . . Card of Pete Rose (100) lists for $45 . . . Complete set lists for $1,000.

1972: There were 16 cards featuring photos of players in their boyhood years . . . Dave Roberts (91) is photo of Danny Coombs . . . Brewers Rookie Card (162) includes photos of Darrell Porter and Jerry Bell, which were reversed . . . Cards of Steve Garvey (686) and Rod Carew (695) list for $60 . . . Card of Pete Rose (559) lists for $50 . . . Complete set lists for $1,000.

1973: A special Home Run Card (1) depicted Babe Ruth, Hank Aaron and Willie Mays . . . Set features rookie card of Mike Schmidt (615) listing for $175 . . . Joe Rudi (360) is photo of Gene Tenace . . . Card of Pete Rose (130) lists for $18 . . . Card of Reggie Jackson (255) lists for $12.50 . . . Complete set lists for $600.

1974: Set features 15 San Diego Padres cards printed as "Washington, N.L." due to report of franchise move, later corrected . . . Also included was a 44-card Traded Series which updated team changes . . . Set features rookie card of Dave Winfield (456) . . . Card of Mike Schmidt (283) lists for $35 . . . Card of Winfield lists for $25 . . . Complete set lists for $325.

1975: Herb Washington (407) is the only card ever published with position "designated runner," featuring only base-running statistics . . . Set features rookie cards of Robin Yount (223), George Brett (228), Jim Rice (616), Gary Carter (620) and Keith Hernandez (623) . . . Don Wilson (455) died after cards went to press (January 5, 1975) . . . Card of Brett lists for $50 . . . Cards of Rice and Carter list for $35 . . . Complete set lists for $475 . . . TOPPS also tested the complete 660-card series in a smaller size (2¼" x 3 1/8") in certain areas of USA in a limited supply . . . Complete set of "Mini-Cards" lists for $700.

1976: As in 1974 there was a 44-card Traded Series . . . Set features five Father & Son cards (66-70) and ten All-Time All-Stars (341-350) . . . Card of Pete Rose (240) lists for $15 . . . Cards

of Jim Rice (340), Gary Carter (441) and George Brett (19) list for $12 . . . Complete set lists for $225.
1977: Set features rookie cards of Andre Dawson (473) and Dale Murphy (476) . . . Reuschel Brother Combination (634) shows the two (Paul and Rick) misidentified . . . Dave Collins (431) is photo of Bob Jones . . . Card of Murphy lists for $65 . . . Card of Pete Rose (450) lists for $8.50 . . . Complete set lists for $250.

1978: Record Breakers (1-7) feature Lou Brock, Sparky Lyle, Willie McCovey, Brooks Robinson, Pete Rose, Nolan Ryan and Reggie Jackson . . . Set features rookie cards of Jack Morris (703), Lou Whitaker (704), Paul Molitor/Alan Trammell (707), Lance Parrish (708) and Eddie Murray (36) . . . Card of Murray lists for $35 . . . Card of Parrish lists for $35 . . . Complete set lists for $200.

1979: Bump Wills (369) was originally shown with Blue Jays affiliation but later corrected to Rangers . . . Set features rookie cards of Ozzie Smith (116), Pedro Guerrero (719), Lonnie Smith (722) and Terry Kennedy (724) . . . Larry Cox (489) is photo of Dave Rader . . . Card of Dale Murphy (39) lists for $8 . . . Cards of Ozzie Smith and Eddie Murray (640) list for $7.50 . . . Complete set lists for $135.

1980: Highlights (1-6) feature Hall-of-Famers Lou Brock, Carl Yastrzemski, Willie McCovey and Pete Rose . . . Set features rookie cards of Dave Stieb (77), Rickey Henderson (482) and Dan Quisenberry (667) . . . Card of Henderson lists for $28 . . . Card of Dale Murphy (274) lists for $5.50 . . . Complete set lists for $135.

1981: Set features rookie cards of Fernando Valenzuela (302), Kirk Gibson (315), Harold Baines (347) and Tim Raines (479) . . . Jeff Cox (133) is photo of Steve McCatty . . . John Littlefield (489) is photo of Mark Riggins . . . Card of Valenzuela lists for $7.50 . . . Card of Raines lists for $9 . . . Complete set lists for $80.

1982: Pascual Perez (383) printed with no position on front lists for $35, later corrected . . . Set features rookie cards of Cal Ripken (21), Jesse Barfield (203), Steve Sax (681) and Kent Hrbek (766) . . . Dave Rucker (261) is photo of Roger Weaver . . . Steve Bedrosian (502) is photo of Larry Owen . . . Card of Ripken lists for $12.50 . . . Cards of Barfield and Sax list for $5 . . . Complete set lists for $75.

1983: Record Breakers (1-6) feature Tony Armas, Rickey Henderson, Greg Minton, Lance Parrish, Manny Trillo and John Wathan . . . A series of Super Veterans features early and current photos of 34 leading players . . . Set features rookie cards of Tony Gwynn (482) and Wade Boggs (498) . . . Card of Boggs lists for $32 . . . Card of Gwynn lists for $16 . . . Complete set lists for $85.

1984: Highlights (1-6) salute eleven different players . . . A parade of superstars is included in Active Leaders (701-718) . . . Set features rookie card of Don Mattingly (8) listing for $35 . . . Card of Darryl Strawberry (182) lists for $10 . . . Complete set lists for $85.

1985: A Father & Son Feature (131-143) is again included . . . Set features rookie cards of Scott Bankhead (393), Mike Dunne (395), Shane Mack (398), John Marzano (399), Oddibe McDowell (400), Mark McGwire (401), Pat Pacillo (402), Cory Snyder (403) and Billy Swift (404) as part of salute to 1984 USA Baseball Team (389-404) that participated in Olympic Games plus rookie cards of Roger Clemens (181) and Eric Davis (627) . . . Card of McGwire lists for $20 . . . Card of Davis lists for $18 . . . Card of Clemens lists for $11 . . . Complete set lists for $95.

1986: Set includes Pete Rose Feature (2-7), which reproduces each of Rose's TOPPS cards from 1963 thru 1985 (four per card) . . . Bob Rodgers (141) should have been numbered 171 . . . Ryne Sandberg (690) is the only card with TOPPS logo omitted . . . Complete set lists for $24.

1987: Record Breakers (1-7) feature Roger Clemens, Jim Deshaies, Dwight Evans, Davey Lopes, Dave Righetti, Ruben Sierra and Todd Worrell . . . Jim Gantner (108) is shown with Brewers logo reversed . . . Complete set lists for $22.

1988: Record Breakers (1-7) include Vince Coleman, Don Mattingly, Mark McGwire, Eddie Murray, Phil & Joe Niekro, Nolan Ryan and Benny Santiago. Al Leiter (18) was originally shown with photo of minor leaguer Steve George and later corrected. Complete set lists for $20.00.

Pitching Record & Index

PLAYER	G	IP	W	L	R	ER	SO	BB	GS	CG	SHO	SV	ERA
AKER, JACK	495	746	47	45			404	274	0	0	0	123	3.28
ALEXANDER, DOYLE	467	2708.1	160	135	1228	1117	1199	803	370	82	13	3	3.71
ALLEN, NEIL	367	793.2	53	58	356	322	508	344	46	7	5	75	3.65
ARMSTRONG, MIKE	167	295.2	18	16			193	138	0	0	0	10	3.71
ARROYO, LUIS	244	533	40	32			336	208	36	10	1	44	3.92
BAHNSEN, STAN	574	2527	146	149			1359	924	327	73	16	20	3.61
BARBER, STEVE	466	1998	121	106			1309	950	272	59	21	13	3.36
BEATTIE, JIM	203	1148.2	52	87	581	532	660	461	182	31	7	1	4.17
BECK, RICH	3	21	2	1			10	7	3	1	1	0	2.14
BEENE, FRED	112	289	12	7			156	111	6	0	0	8	3.61
BIRD, DOUG	432	1213.2	73	60			680	296	100	8	3	60	3.99
BLACKWELL, EWELL	236	1322	82	78			839	562	169	69	16	11	3.30
BLANCO, GIL	28	58	3	5			35	48	9	0	0	0	4.50
BLASINGAME, WADE	222	864	46	51			512	372	128	16	2	5	4.52
BLATERIC, STEVE	5	11	0	0			13	1	0	0	0	0	5.73
BLAYLOCK, GARY	41	126	4	6			81	58	13	3	0	0	4.79
BORDI, RICH	155	330.2	17	18	162	147	218	104	14	0	0	10	4.00
BOUTON, JIM	304	1237	62	63			720	435	144	34	11	6	3.58
BRANCA, RALPH	322	1485	88	68			829	663	188	71	12	19	3.79
BRETT, KEN	349	1526	83	85			807	562	184	51	8	11	3.93
BROWN, HAL	358	1680	85	92			710	389	211	47	13	11	3.81
BURBACH, BILL	37	161	6	11			95	116	28	2	1	0	4.47
BURRIS, RAY	447	2083.2	102	127			1023	720	290	47	10	4	4.10
BUSKEY, TOM	258	480	21	27			212	167	0	0	0	34	3.66
BYRD, HARRY	187	827	46	54			381	355	108	33	8	9	4.35
BYRNE, TOMMY	281	1363	85	69			766	1037	170	65	12	12	4.11
BYSTROM, MARTY	84	435.1	29	26			258	158	79	4	2	0	4.26
CASTRO, BILL	303	545.1	31	26			203	145	9	0	0	45	3.33
CHESBRO, JACK	392	2898	198	130			1265	690	332	261	33	7	2.68
CHRISTIANSEN, CLAY	24	38.2	2	4			27	12	1	0	0	2	6.05
CICOTTE, AL	102	260	10	13			149	119	16	0	0	4	4.36
CLAY, KEN	111	354	10	24			129	141	36	0	0	3	4.68
CLEMENTS, PAT	133	157.1	5	6	57	56	67	72	0	0	0	5	3.20
CLEVENGER, TEX	307	696	36	37			361	298	40	6	2	30	4.18
CLOSTER, ALAN	21	34	2	2			27	43	1	0	0	0	6.88
COATES, JIM	247	683	43	22			396	286	46	13	4	18	4.01
COLEMAN, RIP	95	247	7	25			130	124	33	3	1	5	4.59
COLSON, LOYD	1	2	0	0			3	0	0	0	0	0	4.50
COOPER, DON	37	75.2	1	6			43	43	3	0	0	0	5.23
COWLEY, JOE	90	457.2	33	21	217	199	327	215	72	8	1	0	3.91
COX, CASEY	308	762	39	42			297	234	59	5	0	20	3.70
CULLEN, JACK	19	73	4	4			34	28	9	2	1	1	3.08
CUMBERLAND, JOHN	110	335	15	16			137	103	36	6	2	2	3.81
DALEY, BUD	248	966	60	64			549	351	116	36	3	10	4.03
DAVIS, RON G.	447	692.1	46	52	324	303	550	276	0	0	0	130	3.94
DESHAIES, JIM	30	154	12	6	67	61	135	66	28	1	1	0	3.56
DICKSON, MURRY	625	3053	172	181			1281	1058	338	149	27	23	3.66
DITMAR, ART	287	1267	72	77			552	461	156	41	5	14	3.99
DOBSON, PAT	414	2119	122	129			1301	665	279	74	14	19	3.54
DOWNING, AL	405	2269	123	107			1639	933	327	73	24	3	3.22
DRABEK, DOUG	27	131.2	7	8	64	60	76	50	21	0	0	0	4.10
DREWS, KARL	218	827	44	53			322	332	107	26	7	7	4.76
DUBIEL, WALT	187	880	45	53			289	349	97	41	9	11	3.87
DUREN, RYNE	311	590	27	44			630	392	32	2	1	57	3.83
EASTWICK, RAWLY	326	526	28	27			295	156	1	0	0	68	3.30

PLAYER	G	IP	W	L	R	ER	SO	BB	GS	CG	SHO	SV	ERA
ELLIS, DOCK	345	2129	138	119			1136	674	317	71	14	1	3.45
ERICKSON, ROGER	135	799	35	53			365	251	117	24	0	1	4.13
FERRICK, TOM	323	674	40	40			245	227	7	4	1	56	3.47
FIGUEROA, ED	200	1310	80	68			571	443	179	63	12	1	3.51
FILSON, PETE	126	316.2	14	13			160	121	24	1	0	4	3.95
FISHER, BRIAN	117	195	13	9	93	79	152	66	0	0	0	20	3.65
FONTENOT, RAY	145	493.2	25	26	253	221	216	153	62	3	1	2	4.03
FORD, WHITEY	498	3171	236	106			1956	1086	438	156	45	10	2.74
FRAZIER, GEORGE	361	594.1	30	38	300	270	391	262	0	0	0	27	4.09
FREEMAN, MARK	34	88	3	3			55	38	9	1	0	1	5.52
FRIEND, BOB	602	3612	197	230			1734	894	497	163	36	11	3.58
GARDNER, ROB	109	332	14	18			193	133	42	4	0	2	4.34
GORMAN, TOM A.	289	690	36	36			321	239	33	5	2	42	3.77
GOSSAGE, RICH	725	1482.1	101	89	531	473	1275	592	37	16	0	278	2.87
GRANGER, WAYNE	451	640	35	35			303	201	0	0	0	108	3.14
GRAY, TED	222	1133	59	74			687	595	162	50	7	4	4.37
GRBA, ELI	135	536	23	33			255	284	75	10	0	4	4.48
GRIFFIN, MIKE	41	124.1	4	10			58	37	18	0	0	2	4.49
GRIM, BOB	268	759	61	41			443	330	60	18	4	37	3.62
GUANTE, CECILIO	201	355.2	13	17	139	121	293	136	0	0	0	20	3.06
GUIDRY, RON	334	2219.1	163	80	875	800	1650	580	296	93	26	4	3.24
GULLETT, DON	266	1391	109	50			921	501	184	44	14	11	3.11
GULLICKSON, BILL	213	1430.2	87	73	597	545	799	348	207	37	8	0	3.43
GUMPERT, RANDY	261	1052	51	59			352	346	113	47	6	7	4.17
GURA, LARRY	395	2022	126	94			792	590	257	71	16	13	3.69
HAMBRIGHT, ROGER	18	27	3	1			14	10	0	0	0	3	4.33
HAMILTON, STEVE	421	662	40	31			531	214	17	3	1	42	3.06
HARDIN, JIM	164	752	43	32			408	202	100	28	7	4	3.18
HENRY, BILL F.	2	3	0	0			3	2	0	0	0	0	0.00
HILLER, FRANK	138	533	30	32			197	158	60	22	5	4	4.42
HINTON, RICH	116	250	9	17			152	91	13	2	0	3	4.86
HOGUE, BOBBY	172	327	18	16			108	142	3	0	0	17	3.96
HOLCOMBE, KEN	99	374	18	32			118	170	48	18	2	2	3.99
HOLLAND, AL	356	598.2	33	30			471	214	10	0	0	78	2.72
HOLTZMAN, KEN	451	2868	174	150			1601	910	410	127	31	3	3.49
HOOD, DON	297	847.1	34	35			374	364	72	6	1	6	3.79
HOWELL, JAY	202	390	26	26	184	172	312	146	21	2	0	52	3.97
HUDSON, CHARLES	127	680	32	42	353	301	399	237	105	7	1	0	3.98
HUNTER, JIM	500	3449	224	166			2012	954	476	181	42	1	3.26
JACKSON, GRANT	692	1359	86	75			889	511	83	16	5	79	3.46
JAMES, JOHNNY	66	119	5	3			73	84	3	0	0	2	4.76
JOHN, TOMMY	682	4279.2	264	210	1781	1536	2083	1144	625	159	45	4	3.23
JOHNSON, DON	198	631	27	38			262	285	70	17	4	12	4.78
JOHNSON, KEN	334	1736	91	106			1042	413	331	50	7	9	3.46
JONES, GARY	14	16	0	0			12	8	0	0	0	0	7.87
KAAT, JIM	898	4527.2	283	237			2461	1083	625	180	31	18	3.45
KAUFMAN, CURT	40	86.1	3	3			50	30	1	0	0	1	4.48
KEKICH, MIKE	235	860	39	51			497	442	112	8	1	6	4.59
KEOUGH, MATT	182	1116	53	79			536	476	167	53	7	0	4.19
KING, CLYDE	200	496	32	25			150	189	21	4	0	11	4.14
KIPP, FRED	47	113	6	7			64	48	0	0	0	0	5.10
KLIMKOWSKI, RON	90	186	8	12			79	76	6	1	1	4	2.92
KLINE, STEVE	129	749	43	45			240	184	105	34	6	1	3.27
KONSTANTY, JIM	433	947	66	48			268	269	36	14	2	74	3.46
KRALY, STEVE	5	25	0	2			8	16	3	0	0	1	3.24

PLAYER	G	IP	W	L	R	ER	SO	BB	GS	CG	SHO	SV	ERA
KUCKS, JOHNNY	207	938	54	56			338	308	123	30	7	7	4.10
KUNKEL, BILL	89	143	6	6			83	49	2	0	0	4	4.28
KUZAVA, BOB	213	862	49	44			446	415	99	34	6	13	4.05
LA ROCHE, DAVE	647	1049	65	58			819	459	15	1	0	126	3.53
LARSEN, DON	412	1549	81	91			849	725	171	44	11	23	3.78
LEMON, BOB	460	2849	207	128			1277	1251	350	188	31	22	3.23
LEY, TERRY	6	9	0	0			7	9	0	0	0	0	5.00
LINDBLAD, PAUL	655	1214	68	53			671	444	32	1	1	64	3.25
LINDELL, JOHNNY	55	252	8	18			146	161	28	15	1	1	4.46
LOLLAR, TIM	199	906	47	52	459	430	600	480	131	9	4	4	4.27
LOPAT, EDDIE	340	2439	166	112			859	650	318	164	27	3	3.21
LYLE, SPARKY	899	1390.2	99	76			873	481	0	0	0	238	2.88
MAAS, DUKE	195	734	45	44			356	284	91	21	7	15	4.19
MADISON, DAVE	74	158	8	7			70	103	6	0	0	0	5.70
MAGLIE, SAL	303	1721	119	62			862	652	232	93	25	14	3.15
MAGNUSON, JIM	36	102	2	7			40	41	10	0	0	0	4.59
MARSHALL, CLARENCE	73	185	7	7			69	158	15	1	0	4	5.98
MARTINEZ, TIPPY	543	831	55	42	348	312	629	420	2	0	0	115	3.38
MAY, RUDY	535	2621.1	152	156			1760	958	360	87	24	12	3.46
MCCORMICK, MIKE	484	2381	134	128			1321	795	333	91	33	12	3.73
MCDANIEL, LINDY	987	2140	141	119			1361	623	74	18	2	172	3.45
MCDERMOTT, MICKEY	291	1316	69	69			757	838	156	54	11	14	3.91
MCDEVITT, DANNY	155	456	21	27			303	264	60	13	4	7	4.40
MCDOWELL, SAM	425	2492	141	134			2453	1312	346	103	23	14	3.17
MCGAFFIGAN, ANDY	142	455.1	20	23	188	174	343	151	51	3	1	5	3.44
MCGLOTHEN, LYNN	318	1498	86	93			939	572	201	41	13	2	3.98
MEDICH, GEORGE	312	1995.2	124	105			955	624	287	71	16	2	3.78
MESSERSMITH, ANDY	344	2230	130	99			1625	831	296	103	27	15	2.86
METCALF, TOM	8	13	1	0			3	3	0	0	0	0	2.77
MEYER, BOB	38	129	2	12			92	80	18	3	0	0	4.40
MIKKELSEN, PETE	364	653	45	40			436	250	3	0	0	49	3.38
MILLER, BILL	41	132	6	9			72	79	18	5	2	1	4.23
MIRABELLA, PAUL	156	316.1	11	24			163	161	31	3	1	7	4.92
MONBOUQUETTE, BILL	343	1962	114	112			1122	462	263	78	18	3	3.68
MONROE, ZACK	24	61	4	2			19	29	6	1	0	1	3.39
MONTEFUSCO, JOHN	291	1632	90	83			1076	506	232	31	11	5	3.52
MORGAN, MIKE	101	507	21	45	302	277	228	237	78	14	1	1	4.92
MORGAN, TOM	443	1025	67	47			364	300	61	18	7	64	3.60
MURRAY, DALE	514	898	53	50			400	329	1	0	0	60	3.82
NELSON, GENE	160	528.2	28	34	287	267	305	229	59	6	1	9	4.55
NEWSOM, BOBO	600	3758	211	222			2082	1732	483	246	30	21	3.99
NIEKRO, JOE	670	3426	213	190	1506	1331	1656	1191	472	106	29	16	3.50
NIEKRO, PHIL	838	5265	311	261	2238	1915	3278	1743	690	243	45	29	3.27
NIELSEN, SCOTT	10	56	4	4	29	25	20	12	9	2	2	0	4.02
NOTTEBART, DON	296	927	36	51			525	283	89	16	2	21	3.66
OSTROWSKI, JOE	150	455	23	25			131	98	37	12	0	15	4.55
OVERMIRE, FRANK	266	1130	58	67			301	325	137	50	11	10	3.97
PACELLA, JOHN	69	180.1	4	10			111	120	21	0	0	2	5.84
PAGAN, DAVE	85	232	4	9			143	95	18	3	1	4	4.97
PAGE, JOE	285	790	57	49			519	421	45	14	1	76	3.53
PATTERSON, GIL	10	30	1	2			29	20	6	0	0	1	5.45
PERRY, GAYLORD	777	5352	314	265			3534	1379	690	303	53	11	3.10
PETERSON, FRITZ	355	2216	133	131			1015	426	330	90	20	1	3.30
PILLETTE, DUANE	188	904	38	66			305	391	119	34	4	2	4.40
PORTERFIELD, BOB	318	1568	87	97			572	552	193	92	23	8	3.79
PULIDO, AL	12	34.2	1	1	22	20	16	11	4	0	0	1	5.19
RAJSICH, DAVE	55	115	3	4			76	46	6	0	0	2	4.62
RAMOS, PEDRO	582	2355	117	160			1305	724	268	73	13	55	4.08
RASMUSSEN, DENNIS	81	465	30	17	231	210	317	184	72	6	1	0	4.06
RAWLEY, SHANE	374	1298	81	79	599	548	713	510	137	32	5	40	3..80
REARDON, JEFF	456	665.2	42	46	226	207	537	246	0	0	0	162	2.80
RENIFF, HAL	376	470	21	23			314	242	0	0	0	45	3.27

PLAYER	G	IP	W	L	R	ER	SO	BB	GS	CG	SHO	SV	ERA
REUSCHEL, RICK	436	2771.2	162	155	1195	1056	1652	759	414	81	20	4	3.43
REYNOLDS, ALLIE	434	2492	182	107			1423	1261	309	137	33	49	3.30
RHODEN, RICK	333	2118	121	97	903	818	1177	643	304	60	16	1	3.48
RIGHETTI, DAVE	294	832	58	44	312	278	699	340	76	13	2	107	3.01
RIJO, JOSE	75	319.2	17	23	182	158	288	169	40	4	0	3	4.45
ROBERTS, ROBIN	676	4689	286	245			2357	902	609	305	45	25	3.40
ROLAND, JIM	216	450	19	17			272	229	29	6	1	9	3.22
SAIN, JOHNNY	412	2125	139	116			910	619	245	140	16	51	3.49
SAWYER, RICK	78	206.2	12	9			85	98	20	4	2	0	4.40
SCARBOROUGH, RAY	318	1429	80	85			564	611	168	59	9	14	4.13
SCHMITZ, JOHNNY	366	1813	93	114			746	757	235	86	16	19	3.54
SCHREIBER, PAUL	12	20	0	0			5	10	0	0	0	1	4.05
SCURRY, ROD	293	429.2	19	30	174	152	398	256	7	0	0	37	3.18
SHANTZ, BOBBY	537	1936	119	99			1072	643	171	78	15	48	3.38
SHEA, FRANK	195	944	56	46			361	497	118	48	12	5	3.79
SHELDON, ROLAND	160	725	38	36			371	207	101	17	4	2	4.08
SHIRLEY, BOB	419	1390.1	66	94	657	579	777	521	161	16	2	18	3.75
SHORT, BILL	73	131	5	11			71	64	16	3	1	2	4.74
STAFFORD, BILL	186	786	43	40			449	270	104	18	6	9	3.52
STALEY, GERRY	640	1981	134	111			727	529	186	58	9	61	3.70
STODDARD, TIM	386	560.1	35	30	257	238	459	292	0	0	0	65	3.82
STOTTLEMYRE, MEL	360	2662	164	139			1257	809	356	152	40	1	2.97
STOWE, HAL	1	1	0	0			0	1	0	0	0	0	9.00
STUART, MARLIN	196	486	23	17			185	256	31	7	0	15	4.65
STURDIVANT, TOM	335	1136	59	51			704	449	101	22	7	17	3.75
TALBOT, FRED	195	854	38	56			449	334	126	12	4	1	4.12
TERRY, RALPH	338	1850	107	99			1000	446	257	75	20	11	3.62
TEWKSBURY, BOB	23	130.1	9	5	58	48	49	31	20	2	0	0	3.31
THOMAS, STAN	111	266	11	14			123	110	17	3	0	9	3.69
TIANT, LUIS	573	3485.2	229	172			2416	1104	484	187	49	15	3.30
TIDROW, DICK	620	1747	100	94			967	572	138	33	5	55	3.63
TIEFENAUER, BOB	179	316	9	25			204	87	0	0	0	23	3.84
TILLOTSON, THAD	50	108	4	9			63	46	5	1	0	2	4.08
TORREZ, MIKE	494	3042	185	160			1404	1371	458	117	15	0	3.96
TROUT, DIZZY	521	2726	170	161			1256	1046	322	158	28	35	3.23
TRUCKS, VIRGIL	517	2684	177	135			1534	1088	328	124	33	30	3.38
TURLEY, BOB	310	1711	101	85			1265	1068	237	78	24	12	3.65
TURNER, JIM	231	1132	69	60			329	283	119	69	8	20	3.22
UNDERWOOD, TOM	379	1586.1	86	87			948	662	203	35	6	18	3.89
UPSHAW, CECIL	348	563	34	36			323	177	0	0	0	86	3.13
VERBANIC, JOE	92	207	12	11			94	84	17	3	2	6	3.26
WALLACE, MIKE	123	194	11	3			112	118	4	1	0	3	3.94
WASLEWSKI, GARY	152	411	11	26			229	197	42	5	1	5	3.44
WEHRMEISTER, DAVE	53	118	2	7			64	74	10	0	0	0	6.41
WHITSON, EDDIE	304	1295.1	69	73	642	573	729	477	189	16	6	8	3.98
WIESLER, BOB	70	240	7	19			113	218	38	4	0	0	5.78
WIGHT, BILL	347	1562	77	99			574	714	198	66	15	8	3.95
WILLIAMS, STAN	482	1763	109	94			1305	748	208	42	11	43	3.48
WOMACK, DOOLEY	193	302	19	18			177	111	1	0	0	24	2.95
WOODSON, DICK	137	589	34	32			315	253	76	15	5	2	3.47
WRIGHT, KEN	113	236	11	15			181	180	24	2	1	8	4.54
WYATT, JOHN	435	686	42	44			540	346	9	0	0	103	3.48
WYNNE, BILLY	42	188	8	11			97	78	30	6	1	0	4.31
YORK, JIM	174	285	16	17			194	132	4	0	0	10	3.79

Batting Record & Index

PLAYER	G	AB	R	H	2B	3B	HR	RBI	SB	SLG	BB	SO	AVG
ALLEN, BERNIE	1139	3404	357	815	140	21	73	351	13	.357	360	424	.239
ALOMAR, SANDY	1481	4760	558	1168	126	19	13	282	227	.288	302	482	.245
ALOU, FELIPE	2082	7339	985	2101	359	49	206	852	107	.433	423	706	.286
ALOU, MATTY	1667	5789	780	1777	236	50	31	427	156	.381	311	377	.307
ALSTON, WENDELL	189	332	48	79	7	4	3	35	20	.310	28	44	.238
AMARO, RUBEN	940	2155	211	505	75	13	8	156	11	.292	227	280	.234
ASHFORD, TUCKER	223	510	42	111	31	1	6	55	5	.306	47	75	.218
BAKER, FRANK W.	146	288	28	55	8	3	1	24	4	.250	40	60	.191
BALBONI, STEVE	493	1750	204	412	81	7	100	276	1	.461	155	512	.235
BARKER, RAY	192	318	34	68	16	0	10	44	1	.358	29	76	.214
BAUER, HANK	1544	5145	833	1424	229	57	164	703	50	.439	521	638	.277
BAYLOR, DON	2072	7546	1141	1982	350	28	315	1179	280	.442	726	966	.263
BELLA, ZEKE	52	98	10	18	2	1	1	9	0	.272	10	16	.196
BENIQUEZ, JUAN	1377	4338	581	1193	176	29	70	421	104	.377	325	507	.275
BERBERET, LOU	448	1224	118	281	34	10	31	153	2	.350	200	195	.230
BERGMAN, DAVE	732	1253	151	310	43	10	26	130	13	.360	179	170	.247
BERNHARDT, JUAN	154	492	46	117	19	2	9	43	3	.339	14	40	.238
BERRA, DALE	792	2400	223	570	99	9	47	263	32	.345	193	396	.238
BERRA, YOGI	2120	7555	1175	2150	321	49	358	1430	30	.482	704	414	.285
BLADT, RICH	62	130	14	28	3	1	1	12	6	.277	11	13	.215
BLAIR, PAUL	1946	6042	776	1513	282	55	134	620	171	.382	449	877	.250
BLANCHARD, JOHN	516	1193	137	285	35	2	67	200	2	.441	136	163	.239
BLEFARY, CURT	863	2489	340	583	78	15	101	324	16	.399	456	444	.234
BLOMBERG, RON	461	1333	184	391	67	8	52	224	6	.473	140	134	.293
BOEHMER, LEN	50	116	5	19	4	0	0	7	0	.198	8	10	.163
BOLLWEG, DON	195	452	62	110	22	7	11	53	2	.396	60	68	.243
BONDS, BOBBY	1849	7043	1258	1886	302	66	332	1024	461	.471	914	1757	.268
BONILLA, JUAN	398	1391	139	359	46	9	6	96	7	.317	111	99	.258
BOYER, CLETE	1725	5780	645	1396	200	33	162	654	41	.372	470	931	.242
BRADLEY, SCOTT	105	290	27	80	11	4	5	31	1	.393	15	13	.276
BRICKELL, FRITZ	41	88	7	16	1	0	1	7	0	.227	7	19	.182
BRIDEWESER, JIM	329	620	79	156	22	6	1	50	6	.310	63	78	.252
BRIGHT, HARRY	336	839	99	214	31	4	32	126	2	.416	65	133	.255
BRINKMAN, ED	1845	6045	552	1355	201	38	59	461	30	.299	444	845	.224
BROWN, BOBBY	502	1277	183	313	38	12	26	130	110	.355	94	238	.245
BRYAN, BILL	374	968	86	209	32	9	41	125	0	.395	91	283	.216
CALLISON, JOHNNY	1886	6652	926	1757	321	89	226	840	74	.441	650	1064	.264
CAMPANERIS, BERT	2327	8684	1181	2249	313	86	79	646	649	.342	618	1142	.259
CAREY, ANDY	938	2850	371	741	119	38	64	350	23	.396	268	389	.260
CARMEL, DUKE	124	227	22	48	7	3	4	23	3	.322	27	60	.211
CARROLL, TOM E.	64	30	15	9	0	0	0	1	1	.300	1	6	.300
CATER, DANNY	1289	4451	491	1229	191	29	64	517	26	.375	254	406	.276
CERONE, RICK	858	2796	266	665	126	12	43	304	4	.338	198	290	.238
CERV, BOB	829	2261	320	624	96	26	105	374	12	.481	212	392	.276
CHAMBLISS, CHRIS	2174	7570	912	2109	392	42	185	972	40	.415	632	925	.279
CHAPMAN, BEN	1717	6478	1144	1958	407	107	90	977	287	.440	824	556	.302
CLARK, ALLIE	358	1021	131	267	48	4	32	149	2	.410	72	70	.262
CLARKE, HORACE	1272	4813	548	1230	150	23	27	304	151	.313	365	362	.256
CLINTON, LU	691	2153	270	532	112	31	65	269	12	.418	188	418	.247
COGGINS, RICH	342	1083	125	287	42	13	12	90	50	.361	72	79	.265
COLAVITO, ROCKY	1841	6503	971	1730	283	21	374	1159	19	.489	951	880	.266
COLEMAN, JERRY	723	2119	267	558	77	18	16	217	22	.339	235	218	.263
COLLINS, DAVE	1368	4484	612	1231	171	50	32	344	369	.356	422	594	.275
COLLINS, JOE	908	2329	404	596	79	24	86	329	27	.421	338	263	.256
COMBS, EARLE	1455	5748	1186	1866	309	154	58	629	96	.462	670	278	.325
COTTO, HENRY	174	282	39	74	9	0	2	20	13	.316	15	52	.262

PLAYER	G	AB	R	H	2B	3B	HR	RBI	SB	SLG	BB	SO	AVG
COURTNEY, CLINT	946	2796	260	750	126	17	38	313	3	.366	265	143	.268
COWAN, BILLY	493	1190	131	281	44	8	40	125	17	.387	50	297	.236
COX, BOBBY	220	628	50	141	22	2	9	58	3	.309	75	126	.225
CROSETTI, FRANK	1683	6277	1006	1541	260	65	98	649	113	.354	792	799	.245
DAYETT, BRIAN	121	249	25	61	12	1	9	43	0	.410	17	34	.245
DEJESUS, IVAN	1348	4571	593	1162	175	48	21	323	194	.327	464	657	.254
DEL GRECO, BOBBY	731	1982	271	454	95	11	42	169	16	.352	271	372	.229
DELSING, JIM	822	2461	322	627	112	21	40	286	15	.366	299	251	.255
DEMAESTRI, JOE	1121	3441	322	813	114	23	49	281	15	.325	168	511	.236
DEMPSEY, RICK	1419	3949	438	939	183	12	78	380	17	.349	466	576	.238
DENT, BUCKY	1392	4512	451	1114	169	23	40	423	17	.321	328	350	.247
DICKEY, BILL	1789	6300	930	1969	343	72	202	1209	36	.486	678	289	.313
DOYLE, BRIAN	110	199	18	32	3	0	1	13	1	.191	10	13	.161
DUROCHER, LEO	1637	5350	575	1320	210	56	24	567	31	.320	377	480	.247
EASLER, MIKE	1053	3400	445	1000	179	25	113	491	19	.461	301	644	.294
EDWARDS, DOC	317	906	69	216	33	0	15	87	1	.325	53	109	.238
ELLIS, JOHN	883	2672	259	699	116	13	69	391	6	.392	190	403	.262
ESPINO, JUAN	49	73	2	16	2	0	1	8	0	.288	3	15	.219
EVANS, BARRY	214	501	40	126	17	3	2	41	3	.309	41	62	.251
FERNANDEZ, FRAN	285	727	92	145	21	2	39	116	4	,395	164	231	.199
FERRARO, MIKE	162	500	28	116	18	2	2	30	0	.288	23	61	.232
FISCHLIN, MIKE	516	941	109	207	29	6	3	68	24	.273	92	142	.220
FOLI, TIM	1677	6010	575	1508	241	20	25	499	81	.310	261	397	.251
FOOTE, BARRY	687	2127	191	489	103	10	57	230	10	.368	136	287	.230
GAMBLE, OSCAR	1584	4502	656	1195	188	31	200	666	47	.454	610	546	.265
GARCIA, DAMASO	931	3651	461	1046	173	26	32	301	197	.374	112	292	.286
GARDNER, BILLY	1034	3544	356	841	159	18	41	271	19	.327	246	439	.237
GEHRIG, LOU	2164	8001	1888	2721	535	162	493	1990	102	.632	1510	788	.340
GIBBS, JAKE	538	1639	157	382	53	8	25	146	28	.321	120	231	.233
GONDER, JESSE	395	876	73	220	28	2	26	94	1	.377	72	184	.251
GONZALEZ, FERNANDO	404	1038	85	244	40	7	17	104	7	.336	55	113	.235
GONZALEZ, PEDRO	407	1084	99	264	39	6	8	70	22	.313	52	176	.244
GRIFFEY, KEN	1678	6126	983	1839	315	73	121	707	189	.435	600	750	.300
GULDEN, BRAD	165	413	43	85	14	2	5	42	2	.286	43	56	.206
HADLEY, KENT	171	363	49	88	13	1	14	50	1	.399	30	97	.242
HALE, BOB	376	626	41	171	29	2	2	89	0	.335	26	51	.273
HALL, JIMMIE	968	2848	387	724	100	24	121	391	38	.434	287	529	.254
HANSEN, RON	1384	4311	446	1007	156	17	106	501	9	.351	551	643	.234
HARRAH, TOBY	2155	7402	1115	1954	307	40	195	918	238	.395	1153	868	.264
HART, JIM	1125	3783	518	1052	148	29	170	578	17	.467	380	573	.278
HASSEY, RON	793	2331	249	658	121	7	50	322	10	.405	274	233	.282
HEALY, FRAN	470	1326	144	332	60	6	20	141	30	.350	154	242	.250
HEATH, MIKE	853	2818	316	698	113	20	55	325	38	.361	189	375	.248
HEFFNER, DON	743	2526	275	610	99	19	6	248	18	.303	270	218	.241
HEGAN, MIKE	965	2080	281	504	73	18	53	229	28	.371	311	489	.242
HELD, WOODY	1390	4019	524	963	150	22	179	559	14	.421	509	944	.240
HEMSLEY, ROLLIE	1593	5047	562	1321	257	72	31	555	29	.360	257	395	.262
HENDERSON, RICKEY	1087	4071	862	1182	188	39	103	417	660	.432	708	562	.290
HENDRICKS, ELLIE	711	1888	205	415	66	7	62	230	1	.361	229	319	.220
HERNANDEZ, LEO	66	205	21	50	6	1	6	26	1	.371	12	21	.244
HERRMANN, ED	922	2729	247	654	92	4	80	320	6	.364	260	361	.240
HOBSON, BUTCH	738	2556	314	634	107	23	98	397	11	.423	183	569	.248
HOPP, JOHNNY	1393	4260	698	1262	216	74	46	458	128	.414	465	378	.296
HOUK, RALPH	91	158	12	43	6	1	0	20	0	.323	12	10	.272
HOWARD, ELSTON	1605	5363	619	1471	218	50	167	762	9	.427	373	786	.274

PLAYER	G	AB	R	H	2B	3B	HR	RBI	SB	SLG	BB	SO	AVG
HOWSER, DICK	789	2483	398	617	90	17	16	165	105	.318	367	186	.248
HUNT, KEN L.	310	782	107	177	42	4	33	111	9	.417	85	222	.226
HUNTER, BILLY	630	1875	166	410	58	18	16	144	23	.294	111	192	.219
JACKSON, REGGIE	2705	9528	1509	2510	449	48	548	1659	226	.493	1342	2500	.263
JAVIER, STAN	66	121	14	24	8	0	0	8	8	.264	16	28	.198
JENSEN, JACKIE	1438	5236	810	1463	259	45	199	929	143	.460	750	546	.279
JIMENEZ, ELVIO	1	6	0	2	0	0	0	0	0	.333	0	0	.333
JOHNSON, ALEX	1322	4623	550	1331	180	33	78	525	103	.392	244	626	.288
JOHNSON, BILLY	964	3253	419	882	141	33	61	487	13	.391	347	290	.271
JOHNSON, CLIFF	1369	3945	539	1016	198	10	196	699	9	.462	568	719	.258
JOHNSON, DARRELL	134	320	24	75	6	1	2	28	1	.278	26	39	.234
JOHNSON, DERON	1765	5941	706	1447	247	33	245	923	11	.420	587	1318	.244
JOHNSTONE, JAY	1748	4703	578	1254	215	38	102	531	50	.394	429	632	.267
JONES, DARRYL	18	47	6	12	5	1	0	6	0	.404	2	7	.255
JONES, RUPPERT	1246	4223	618	1056	207	36	139	551	141	.415	514	779	.250
KEANE, JOHNNY	No major league statistics												
KEMP, STEVE	1139	4006	578	1117	179	25	129	631	37	.433	570	590	.279
KENNEDY, JOHN	856	2110	237	475	77	17	32	185	14	.323	142	461	.225
KENNEY, JERRY	465	1369	165	325	38	13	7	103	59	.299	184	139	.237
KINGMAN, DAVE	1941	667	901	1575	240	25	442	1210	85	.478	608	1816	.236
KITTLE, RON	536	1770	238	408	61	3	115	299	16	.463	157	501	.231
KLUTTS, MICKEY	199	536	49	129	26	1	4	59	1	.315	34	101	.241
KOSCO, ANDY	658	1963	204	464	75	8	73	267	5	.394	99	350	.236
KRYHOSKI, DICK	569	1794	203	475	85	14	45	231	5	.403	119	163	.265
KUBEK, TONY	1092	4167	522	1109	178	30	57	373	29	.364	217	441	.266
LANIER, HAL	1196	3703	297	843	111	20	8	273	11	.275	136	436	.228
LEFEBVRE, JOE	433	1073	139	279	52	13	31	130	11	.419	136	199	.260
LEJA, FRANK	26	23	3	1	0	0	0	0	0	.043	1	8	.043
LEON, EDDIE	601	1862	165	440	51	10	24	159	7	.313	156	358	.236
LINZ, PHIL	519	1372	185	322	64	4	11	96	13	.311	112	195	.235
LITTLE, BRYAN	293	846	120	212	35	5	3	75	8	.314	114	68	.251
LOCKLEAR, GENE	292	595	76	163	24	2	9	66	13	.373	55	87	.274
LOLLAR, SHERMAN	1752	5351	623	1415	244	14	155	808	20	.402	671	453	.264
LONG, DALE	1013	3020	384	805	135	33	132	467	0	.464	353	460	.267
LOPEZ, ART	38	49	5	7	0	0	0	0	0	.143	1	6	.143
LOPEZ, HECTOR	1451	4644	623	1251	193	37	136	591	16	.415	418	696	.269
LUMPE, JERRY	1371	4912	620	1314	190	52	47	454	20	.356	428	411	.268
LYTTLE, JIM	391	710	71	176	37	5	9	70	4	.352	61	139	.248
MADDOX, ELLIOTT	1029	2843	360	742	121	16	18	234	60	.334	409	358	.261
MAJESKI, HANK	1069	3421	404	956	181	27	57	501	10	.398	299	260	.279
MANTLE, MICKEY	2401	8102	1677	2415	344	72	536	1509	153	.557	1734	1710	.298
MAPES, CLIFF	459	1193	199	289	55	13	38	172	8	.406	168	213	.242
MARIS, ROGER	1463	5101	826	1325	195	42	275	851	21	.476	652	733	.260
MARTIN, BILLY	1021	3419	425	877	137	28	64	333	34	.369	187	355	.257
MASON, JIM	633	1584	140	322	53	12	12	114	2	.275	124	316	.203
MATTINGLY, DON	572	2223	349	737	160	11	93	401	3	.539	171	141	.332
MAY, CARLOS	1165	4120	544	1127	172	23	90	536	85	.392	512	565	.274
MAYBERRY, JOHN	1620	5447	733	1379	211	19	255	879	20	.439	881	810	.253
MAZZILLI, LEE	1243	3758	514	987	176	23	84	406	183	.389	555	562	.263
MCDONALD, DAVE	33	62	3	9	3	0	1	6	0	.242	6	19	.145
MCDOUGALD, GIL	1336	4676	697	1291	187	51	112	576	45	.410	559	623	.276
MCKINNEY, RICH	341	886	79	199	28	2	20	100	4	.328	77	124	.225
MEACHAM, BOBBY	333	1053	156	244	38	7	3	86	45	.290	107	221	.232
MICHAEL, GENE	973	2806	249	642	86	12	15	226	22	.284	234	421	.229
MILBOURNE, LARRY	989	2448	290	623	71	24	11	184	41	.317	133	176	.254
MILLER, JOHN A.	32	61	4	10	1	0	2	3	0	.279	2	18	.164
MILLS, BUSTER	415	1379	200	396	62	19	14	163	24	.390	131	137	.287
MIRANDA, WILLIE	824	1914	176	423	50	14	6	132	13	.271	165	250	.221
MITCHELL, BOBBY VANCE	273	609	86	143	29	6	21	91	14	.406	56	168	.235
MIZE, JOHNNEY	1884	6443	1118	2011	367	83	359	1337	28	562	856	524	.312

PLAYER	G	AB	R	H	2B	3B	HR	RBI	SB	SLG	BB	SO	AVG
MOORE, ARCHIE	40	40	5	11	4	0	1	5	0	.450	6	13	.275
MORENO, OMAR	1382	4992	699	1257	171	87	37	386	487	.343	387	885	.252
MOSCHITTO, ROSS	110	36	13	6	0	0	1	3	0	.250	1	14	.167
MOSES, GERRY	385	1072	89	269	48	8	25	109	1	.381	63	184	.251
MUMPHREY, JERRY	1404	4618	616	1330	196	53	57	522	173	.390	436	625	.288
MUNSON, THURMAN	1423	5344	696	1558	229	32	113	701	49	.410	438	570	.292
MURCER, BOBBY	1908	6730	972	1862	285	45	252	1043	128	.445	862	841	.277
MURRAY, LARRY	226	412	49	73	16	4	3	31	20	.257	49	74	.177
NARRON, JERRY	388	832	64	177	23	2	21	96	0	.321	67	125	.213
NETTLES, GRAIG	2508	8716	1172	2172	316	27	384	1267	31	.424	1057	1165	.249
NIARHOS, GUS	315	691	114	174	26	5	1	59	6	.308	153	56	.252
NIXON, OTIS	271	362	85	79	8	1	3	18	57	.271	30	55	.218
NOREN, IRV	1093	3119	443	857	157	35	65	453	34	.410	335	350	.275
O'BERRY, MIKE	177	355	36	68	10	1	3	28	0	.251	39	74	.192
O'NEILL, STEVE	1586	4795	448	1259	248	34	13	537	30	.337	592	283	.263
OATES, JOHNNY	593	1637	146	410	56	2	14	126	11	.313	141	149	.250
OFFICE, ROWLAND	899	2413	259	626	101	11	32	242	27	.350	189	311	.259
OLIVER, BOB	847	2914	293	745	102	19	94	419	17	.400	156	562	.256
OLIVER, NATE	410	954	107	216	24	5	2	45	17	.268	72	172	.226
PAGLIARULO, MIKE	354	1085	150	259	55	8	54	167	4	.453	114	252	.239
PASQUA, DAN	162	428	61	113	20	1	25	70	2	.491	63	116	.264
PEPITONE, JOE	1397	5097	606	1315	158	35	219	721	41	.432	302	526	.258
PEREZ, MARTY	931	3131	313	771	108	22	22	241	11	.316	245	369	.246
PHILLIPS, JACK	343	892	111	252	42	16	9	101	5	.396	85	86	.283
PINIELLA, LOU	1747	5867	651	1705	305	41	102	766	33	.409	368	541	.291
PISONI, JIM	103	189	26	40	3	3	6	20	0	.354	16	47	.212
PRIDDY, GERRY	1296	4720	612	1252	232	46	61	541	44	.373	624	639	.265
RAMOS, BOBBY	103	232	20	44	7	1	4	17	0	.280	22	38	.190
RAMOS, DOMINGO	250	517	50	108	16	0	3	33	5	.257	42	67	.209
RANDLE, LEN	1138	3950	488	1016	145	40	27	322	156	.335	372	505	.257
RANDOLPH, WILLIE	1494	5511	897	1511	216	55	39	451	233	.355	875	454	.274
REESE, JIMMIE	232	742	123	206	39	4	8	70	7	.373	48	37	.278
RENNA, BILL	370	918	123	219	36	10	28	119	2	.391	99	166	.239
REPOZ, ROGER	831	2145	257	480	73	19	82	260	26	.390	280	499	.224
REVERING, DAVE	557	1832	205	486	83	16	62	234	6	.430	148	240	.265
RICHARDSON, BOBBY	1412	5386	643	1432	196	37	34	390	73	.335	262	243	.266
RIVERS, MICKEY	1467	5629	785	1660	247	71	61	499	267	.397	266	471	.295
RIZZUTO, PHIL	1661	5816	877	1588	239	62	38	563	149	.355	650	397	.273
ROBERTSON, ANDRE	254	724	80	182	32	4	5	54	4	.327	26	120	.251
ROBINSON, BILL	1472	4364	536	1127	229	29	166	641	71	.438	263	819	.258
ROBINSON, BRUCE	38	101	5	23	3	1	0	10	0	.277	4	12	.228
ROBINSON, EDDIE	1314	4279	545	1145	171	24	172	723	10	.439	520	359	.268
RODRIGUEZ, AURELIO	2017	6611	612	1570	287	46	124	648	35	.351	324	943	.237
RODRIGUEZ, ELLIE	7795	2173	220	533	76	6	16	203	17	.308	332	291	.245
ROENICKE, GARY	947	2443	331	611	122	4	111	375	16	.440	366	390	.250
ROLFE, RED	1175	4827	942	1394	257	67	69	497	44	.413	526	335	.289
ROYSTER, JERRY	1287	3910	518	979	149	33	33	324	185	.331	382	486	.250
RUTH, BABE	2503	8397	2174	2873	506	136	714	2204	123	.690	2056	1330	.342
SAKATA, LENN	529	1210	154	272	44	3	23	100	30	.323	92	148	.225
SALAS, MARK	225	638	80	170	28	9	17	75	3	.418	36	72	.266
SAMPLE, BILLY	826	2516	371	684	127	9	46	230	98	.384	195	230	.272
SANCHEZ, CELERINO	105	314	30	76	11	3	1	31	1	.306	14	42	.242
SANDS, CHARLIE	93	145	15	31	6	1	6	23	0	.393	36	35	.214
SCHMIDT, BOB	454	1305	133	317	55	4	39	150	0	.381	100	199	.243
SCHOFIELD, J. DICK	1321	3083	394	699	113	20	21	211	12	.297	390	526	.227
SCHULT, ART	164	421	58	111	24	0	6	56	0	.363	23	50	.264
SCOTT, GEORGE	2034	7433	957	1992	306	60	271	1051	69	.435	699	1418	.268
SCOTT, RODNEY	690	2132	316	504	43	26	3	150	205	.285	281	291	.236
SHOPAY, TOM	253	309	40	62	7	1	3	20	11	.259	26	51	.201
SIEBERN, NORM	1406	4481	662	1217	206	38	132	636	18	.423	708	749	.272

PLAYER	G	AB	R	H	2B	3B	HR	RBI	SB	SLG	BB	SO	AVG
SILVERA, CHARLIE	227	482	34	136	15	2	1	52	2	.328	53	32	.282
SIMPSON, DICK	288	518	94	107	19	2	15	56	10	.338	64	174	.207
SIMPSON, HARRY	888	2829	343	752	101	41	73	381	17	.408	271	429	.266
SIMS, DUKE	843	2422	263	580	80	6	100	310	6	.401	338	483	.239
SKINNER, JOEL	185	450	38	108	15	2	6	46	2	322	28	116	.240
SKIZAS, LOU	239	725	80	196	27	4	30	86	8	.443	50	37	.270
SKOWRON, BILL	1658	5547	681	1566	243	53	211	888	16	.459	383	870	.282
SLAUGHTER, ENOS	2380	7946	1247	2383	413	148	169	1304	71	.453	1019	538	.300
SMALLEY, ROY JR.	1543	5348	713	1369	228	24	155	660	25	.395	735	856	.256
SMITH, CHARLIE	771	2484	228	594	83	18	69	281	7	.370	130	565	.239
SODERHOLM, ERIC	894	2894	402	764	120	14	102	383	18	.421	295	359	.264
SOLAITA, TONY	525	1316	164	336	66	1	50	203	2	.421	214	345	.255
SOUCHOCK, STEVE	473	1227	163	313	58	20	50	186	15	.457	88	164	.255
SPENCER, JIM	1553	4908	541	1227	179	27	146	599	11	.387	407	582	.250
SPIKES, CHARLIE	670	2039	240	502	72	12	65	256	27	.389	154	388	.246
STAIGER, ROY	152	457	42	104	19	1	4	38	4	.300	30	59	.228
STANLEY, FRED	815	1650	197	356	38	5	10	120	11	.263	196	243	.216
STEGMAN, DAVE	171	320	39	66	10	2	8	32	5	.325	31	55	.206
STENGEL, CASEY	1277	4288	575	1219	182	89	60	535	131	.410	437	453	.284
STEWART, ED	773	2041	288	547	96	32	32	260	29	.393	252	157	.268
STIRNWEISS, GEORGE	1028	3695	604	989	157	68	29	281	134	.371	541	447	.268
SUDAKIS, BILL	530	1548	177	362	56	7	59	214	9	.393	169	313	.234
SWOBODA, RON	927	2581	285	624	87	24	73	344	20	.379	299	647	.242
TEPEDINO, FRANK	265	507	50	122	13	1	6	58	4	.306	33	61	.241
THOMAS, LEE	1027	3324	405	847	111	22	106	428	25	.397	332	397	.255
THOMASSON, GARY	901	2373	315	591	103	25	61	294	50	.391	291	463	.249
THRONEBERRY, MARV	480	1186	143	281	37	8	53	170	3	.416	130	295	.237
TILLMAN, BOB	775	2329	189	540	68	10	79	282	1	.371	228	510	.232
TOLLESON, WAYNE	568	1700	217	433	48	14	7	93	96	.312	146	256	.255
TORGESON, EARL	1668	4969	848	1318	215	46	149	740	133	.417	980	653	.265
TORRES, RUSTY	654	1314	159	279	45	5	35	126	13	.334	164	246	.212
TOVAR, CESAR	1488	5569	834	1546	253	55	46	435	226	.368	413	410	.278
TRESH, TOM	1192	4251	595	1041	179	34	153	530	45	.411	550	698	.245
TRIANDOS, GUS	1206	3907	389	954	147	6	167	608	1	.413	440	636	.244
VALO, ELMER	1806	5029	768	1420	228	73	58	601	110	.391	943	284	.282
VELEZ, OTTO	637	1802	244	452	87	11	78	272	6	.441	336	414	.251
VIRDON, BILL	1583	5980	735	1596	237	81	91	502	47	.379	442	647	.267
WALKER, DIXIE	1905	6740	1037	2064	376	96	105	1023	59	.437	817	325	.306
WALTON, DANNY	297	779	69	174	27	4	28	107	4	.376	88	240	.223
WARD, GARY	831	3118	444	900	144	36	92	419	71	.446	240	524	.289
WARD, PETE	973	3060	345	776	136	17	98	427	20	.405	371	539	.254
WASHINGTON, CLAUDELL	1529	5488	762	1524	275	61	130	665	270	.421	386	1029	.278
WATSON, BOB	1832	6185	802	1826	307	41	184	989	27	.447	653	796	.295
WERTH, DENNIS	117	139	28	29	4	0	3	15	1	.288	24	33	.209
WHITAKER, STEVE	266	758	73	174	20	6	24	85	4	.367	54	174	.230
WHITE, ROY	1881	6650	964	1803	300	51	160	758	232	.404	934	708	.271
WHITFIELD, TERRY	711	1899	233	536	93	12	33	179	18	.396	133	286	.282
WILBORN, TED	30	20	5	2	0	0	0	1	0	.100	1	8	.100
WILLIAMS, WALT	842	2373	284	640	106	11	33	173	34	.365	126	211	.270
WILSON, ARCHIE	51	140	9	31	5	3	0	17	0	.300	7	14	.221
WINDHORN, GORDON	95	108	20	19	9	1	2	8	1	.333	11	19	.176
WINFIELD, DAVE	1964	7287	1135	2083	353	71	305	1234	195	.479	791	1040	.286
WOODLING, GENE	1796	5587	830	1585	257	63	147	830	29	.431	920	477	.284
WOODS, RON	582	1247	162	290	34	12	26	130	27	.342	175	171	.233
WYNEGAR, BUTCH	1243	4183	486	1069	170	14	64	493	10	.349	609	408	.256
WYNN, JIM	1920	6653	1105	1665	285	39	291	964	225	.436	1224	1427	.250
ZEBER, GEORGE	28	71	8	21	3	0	3	10	0	.465	9	11	.296
ZUVELLA, PAUL	118	269	20	57	10	1	0	7	2	.257	25	22	.212